THE
UNKNOWN
PILGRIM

THE UNKNOWN PILGRIM

The Soul's Journey to God
and to the Holy Mountain of Athos

RENÉ GOTHÓNI

MANTON, CALIFORNIA

2006

The Unknown Pilgrim
English Translation © 2006 by René Gothóni.

ISBN 10 digit: 0-9714139-3-2

Published by Divine Ascent Press
P. O. Box 439
21770 Ponderosa Way
Manton, California 96059
www.divineascent.org

Divine Ascent Press is the publishing arm of the
Monastery of Saint John of San Francisco
www.monasteryofstjohn.org

Originally published in Finnish as *Tuntematon pyhiinvaeltaja* © 2000
WSOY. Helsinki, Finland.

Scripture taken from the *Revised English Bible*, Oxford and Cambridge UP, 1989
Used by permission. All rights reserved.

Cover illustration taken from the 1688 publication
Isola Dirodi: Geographica—Storica, Antica, e Moderna, Coll' Altre Adiacenti
Già possedute da Caualieri Hospitalieri di S. Giouanni di Gerusalemme.
Opera de Padri Mæstri Coronelli

PRINTED AND BOUND IN THE UNITED STATES OF AMERICA
BY VERSA PRESS, INC.

Dedicated To

Jennifer and Graham Speake

Contents

THE
UNKNOWN
PILGRIM

PART ONE

Ouranoupolis

The Tower

I

THERE ARE FEWER TOURISTS AT this time of the year. I know this from the field-work I have done here every September since 1984. Most Europeans, whether continental or British, have already taken their summer holidays in late July or August, normally the warmest time of the year all over Europe. By October everyone has returned to work. Their own countries are again functioning at full working capacity.

Gone are the German groups whose money the *taverna-keepers* await greedily as they sit in their blue chairs outside their houses, still seeking revenge for the havoc the Nazis wreaked in the village nearly sixty years ago. Memories are long. Gone also are the Italian families; the elderly British couples; the pairs of Austrians; the Americans, the Canadians and the French, who nearly always arrive single as do the Scandinavian girls; and then, of course, the middle-aged Greek couples amusing themselves on late-summer weekends, cheerfully dangling their feet in the water, occasionally shouting to each other "*poly kryo*" ("very cold water") as they head for a swim in their beloved sea, the *thálassa*. They cleanse not only their bodies, but also their souls of the noise and petrol fumes that pollute the city of Thessalonica. Only some Russians, Romanians and other nouveau-riche from Eastern Europe pop in unexpectedly for a few days, unfolding their huge parasols, reminiscent of upper-class ladies of the late 19th century, relaxing on the beach. They watch the afternoon ferries and ships that come and go at the jetty of Ouranoupolis, the last station in the world for pilgrims to enter the monastic republic known to all Greeks simply as the Holy Mountain (*Agion Oros*).

It is the easternmost peninsula of the three Chalkidikian fingers rising majestically from the Aegean Sea.

Gone forever from the row of seaside *tavernas* are this year's laughing and babbling crowds. The futile tans of thousands of tourists are inevitably fading away, like their footprints on the sand wiped out long ago by the waves lapping the beach. Life is transitory! But the tower remains at the tip of the seafront like the exclamation mark at the end of the evocative maxim: *memento mori!*

Few are the signs of life along the winding seashore—merely the occasional *taverna*-keeper sipping his morning coffee outside his partly closed eating establishment. The cement terraces are mostly empty, since the chairs and tables have long ago been stored away for the winter. The bare ground hints at the populous life at the *tavernas* only to someone who knows the seasons of the seaside village. Casual passers-by standing in front of the deserted seashore cannot in their wildest dreams imagine the easy-going and picturesque summer evenings here.

The souvenir shops are closed, as if in hibernation. Only a few kiosks by the jetty stay open all year round to cater to pilgrims and Athonite monks, as do the bakery and the biggest supermarket serving the villagers. A few *tavernas* provide travellers with meals, often taken inside in the chilly evenings, but most of the time the Greek eating establishment functions as a meeting place for local men whiling away their winter days. In mid-October, the season is definitely over.

Any observant connoisseur of Greek culture may notice elderly men appearing here and there with the morning sun as they join the *taverna*-keepers outside their closed businesses to chit-chat about their lives as they revive their bodies, stiff after the cold night, with strong Greek coffee. They exchange views on current affairs, incessantly playing with their strings of beads (*kombológia*), twisting the string up and off around their forefingers while listening to each other's opinions. This habit, second nature to them, is about to disappear. The younger men in the village have traded the string of beads for cigarettes, which they tend to smoke constantly, especially on bleak mornings like these, harbingers of the coming winter. As soon as they have finished one cigarette they immediately light another, which they usually put on the ashtray for a while. A cigarette is always burning like incense, ready to be taken up at will. The nervous tension, which was always relieved by twisting the string of beads or occasionally by praying for mercy, *"Kyrie, eleison"*—in the traditional Orthodox style—is now fed by this obsessive smoking. Apart from being unhealthy, it is also a completely vain and profane habit. Christos, one of the few non-smoking middle-aged men in the village, suddenly turned up, as it seemed, from nowhere.

"*Yásu* (Hello) Renéos!" he said with surprised delight, "You're back again—writing in your diary."

"Writing is my way of life," I responded spontaneously, and asked him to sit down as Greeks always do. *"Katse lígo, katse* (Sit down for a while). Where did you appear from?"

"I'm going to my mother's house," he explained. "Look at these fresh fish I caught early this morning." He was full of pride as he showed me the plastic bag full of fish.

Christos is an old friend of mine. He is the engineer in the village. His main hobby is fishing. Whenever he is free or whenever he thinks the weather is good enough he goes out with his bait. He usually catches a lot of fish, and always gives some to his mother, who was left a widow very young during the civil war.

Christos' mother has a large house by the sea on the other side of the village. For years she has rented the rooms on the second floor to tourists and pilgrims for a night or two as they wait to catch the ferry the next morning to the Holy Mountain of Athos. Athos, by the way, is considered to be the oldest continuing democracy in existence. Athonite monks also stay at her house from time to time. There are only two ferries a day to the Holy Mountain, both departing early in the morning.

Christos' mother is devout Orthodox, as indeed are most of the villagers. She always gives Athonites a free meal, suitable for a monastic: fresh vegetables, bread, fish and olives, all washed down with the best Athonite wine that Christos has brought back from the monasteries in exchange for servicing various machines there.

"It's nice to be back again by the tower," I said, thrilled to meet my old friend.

"Are you renting the same room this year too?" he asked, as the villagers always do. They want to know where you are staying. If possible, they also want to know how much you pay per night. This is a way of keeping prices at the same level. I told him that I enjoyed my room, and especially the view from the balcony.

"When are you going to the Holy Mountain?" he asked, taking it for granted that I would be going there.

"This time I came here for another reason." Not wanting to go into details in front of the other men, I diverted his attention.

"When did you say the tower was built?"

"Don't you remember? I told you last year that it was erected by Andronicos the Second, the Byzantine emperor, sometime in the middle of the 14th century. At that time the whole area was farmland, with vineyards that belonged to the monastery of Vatopedi. That's one of the oldest ruling monasteries on the Holy Mountain."

"Ouranoupolis, 'the City of the Sky,' is an apt name for the last outpost of the 'world,' the *kosmos.*"

"How true. It's the end of the *kosmos* as we know it," Christos reminded me. "How long are you staying this time?"

The other men had already left our company so I confessed: "I was utterly fed up with my work. I needed to get away from all of my obligations—so—I prescribed myself a fortnight's sabbatical. With no further ado I packed my bags and here I am!"

"You did the right thing. Are you writing a new book?" Christos did not realize how burnt out I was.

"I came only to relax and to listen to the sounds of silence."

"You're right. Life in the village has certainly quieted down since last week. This is a good time for you to be here."

"What are you doing this evening?" I asked.

"Getting ready for tomorrow. I'm taking the seven o'clock ferry to the monastery of Dionysiou for two days. Do you know the monastery?"

"What are you going to do there?"

"Father Paisios asked me to put up some solar panels outside his *kellion*. He's already quite old and the oil lamps are dangerous. Did you know that Father Nikon's house burnt to the ground last winter? The flame from the lamp suddenly set the wall alight while he was having his afternoon nap."

"What about Father Nikon?" I asked anxiously.

"Miraculously the smoke woke him up and he managed to get out just in time. The flames destroyed the whole interior. After that incident the *hegumenos* decided to install solar panels to get electricity into the *kellia* inhabited by old monks."

"Aren't the panels expensive?"

"The monastery got funds from the EU to restore the old buildings. They have been falling into decay for decades," he explained. "The roofs in particular need to be fixed. There are large holes everywhere. Restoration work is in progress in most of the monasteries these days."

"Some of the monasteries badly need looking after," I agreed.

"Well, Renéos, I'll have to go now. Come and have lunch at my house on Saturday when I'm back from Dionysiou."

"Should I come about one o'clock as usual?"

"Do that. See you then." He got up from the chair and headed towards his mother's house. "The beach is all yours. Don't burn yourself!" He was still shouting as he disappeared behind the house at the corner of the street.

Last year Christos told me that Ouranoupolis was a village no more than eighty years old. It was founded in the early 1920s, when about six hundred families from the Princes' Isles, Smyrna and Caesarea settled near the tower as one and a half million Greeks were forced to leave Asia Minor. This was the effect of the exchange-of-population treaty between Turkey and Greece. In great haste, the Greek state built small houses with gardens for the migrants, expecting them to grow their own produce. Christos' parents came from the Princes' Isles. They were fishermen, while those from Caesarea and Smyrna were rug makers. However, the Greek authorities assumed that the migrants would take up farming and thereby become self-sufficient. Accordingly, each family was given a piece of farmland on the hillside outside the village proper.

The harvest was poor. In order to survive, the villagers planted olive groves and vineyards. Every family had a few goats and sheep to give them milk, cheese and meat. Their main sources of income were fishing and seasonal work on the Holy Mountain. There the men picked olives, chestnuts and hazelnuts, harvested grapes and gathered vegetables. This gave work to half the men in the village. In the autumn they also worked in the forests, which were a profitable asset of the monasteries. This was how the village of Prosphorion was established and organized during its first decades.

Prosphorá means "gift," and the area was then known as Prosphorion. The tower and its storehouse are the oldest buildings in the village. At the top of the tower is a small chapel. The double-headed eagle carved on the floor tells us that the Byzantine emperor had the tower built to shelter the monks and workers from pirates, who constantly tried to rob the monasteries of their food supplies and treasures.

In the early 1960s, the name of the village was changed to Pirgos, which literally means "tower." This was considered a more appropriate way to attract tourists. It was renamed Ouranoupolis a few years later, when it turned out that there were many villages in Greece named Pirgos. Archeologists had discovered the remains of an ancient town called Ouranoupolis on the mountain nearby, apparently founded at the time of Alexander the Great. This was a compelling reason for using the name again...

The Greeks are aware and proud of their ancient past and proud of it. The leaders of most of the so-called new villages established in the 1920s have studied the history of their own area with a view to rooting the present in the glorious past and creating continuity between the two. Ouranoupolis, "the City of the Sky," also serves as a ladder to the future. It is the last outpost of the world, and the jetty is the sacred bridge to the Holy Mountain of Athos, the seat of angelic life on earth.

AFTER MY STROLL ON THE BEACH, a salad for lunch and a brief afternoon nap—a habit that always forces itself on me during my first few days in Greece—I went to visit Martha from Switzerland, who has lived in the village since 1954. As I often do, I bought some cakes on my way to her house for our five o'clock tea, another habit of mine before I leave for the Holy Mountain. According to Martha, it was the Australian-English couple Joice and Sydney Loch who kept the village together during its first two decades. They had joined the Quaker relief mission in Poland in 1922, where they discovered their true vocation: service to others. Their work then took them to northern Greece to help settle the forced migrants from Asia Minor.

Eventually, because of the shortage of accommodation, they ended up living in the tower. It soon became the center of activities aimed at improving the living conditions in the village. There was no doctor. Mrs. Loch became the surrogate GP: she ordered the medicines, acted as midwife, sewed up wounds and occasionally she even did major surgery. She later received the Red Cross Medal for her activities.

Life in the village was hard at the beginning. It can with reason be compared with the spiritual struggle of the Athonites. The winters were dark and cold. The houses were heated by wood-burning stoves, but there was not much fuel around. Bread and other food scarcely lasted the winter. Olive oil was particularly important in disease prevention. Many people went hungry and suffered from malaria.

There was only one well in the village, and no electricity or water in the houses. As if in answer to a prayer, Mrs. Loch sold one of her children's books in America, and the money she received enabled her to pay for the digging of eight wells in the village. The English Quakers sent the pipes, and an engineer from the Farm School near Thessalonica laid them into the earth with the help of some of the bigger boys in the village.

Over the years, Mrs. Loch became regarded as the mother of the village. She helped those in need and was a great source of consolation. Her home in the tower also became a place for many an Athos pilgrim to rest. There was no other place to stay overnight. Through her husband she got to know some of the monks. The famous Russian, Father Nikon, was like a spiritual father to both of them.

No wonder the villagers grew very fond of the couple. Sydney Loch died suddenly in February 1954, but Joice lived another 30 years in the village, editing her husband's Athos book and writing her autobiography. When she died in 1982, the entire village took part in the funeral. Christos told me that it is still remembered as the most moving funeral they had ever had.

Here in Greece, bodily remains are dug up three years after death. The bones and the skull are washed with wine and then placed in a special building in the cemetery next to the chapel, which in Ouranoupolis is dedicated to St. John the Theologian. The grave of Joice and Sydney Loch is an exception to the rule. It is preserved as in England.

Before sunset I went to pay my respects to both of them, yet another habit of mine. I stood for a while at their grave, pondering: life is short. It may contain much suffering and grief, but there is also hope and progress. Ouranoupolis is blooming today, thanks largely to Joice and Sydney Loch.

Martha told me that life in this outlying village was practically unchanged until the 1960s. The first telephone network was established in the middle of the 1950s. It was only in 1963 that the village became part of the Greek tourist industry. It was then that the road from Tripiti was extended to the village in order to enable the delegates to take part in the celebrations of the millennium of monasticism on the Holy Mountain. Electricity was brought to the village as the road work proceeded.

Since the 1960s, many young people have spent the winter in Germany, working in restaurants, on building sites and in other service jobs. They come home for the summer with fancy motorcycles and cars, bringing money and ideas about how to attract tourists to the village.

The first hotels were built in the early 1970s, along with supermarkets, restaurants, pubs, discos and souvenir shops. Fast-food restaurants came in 1988. The poor village was thus gradually transformed into a relatively wealthy place, thanks to the tourists. Today it is almost entirely dependent on vacationers, which makes it vulnerable at times of unrest in Europe. The conflict in the Balkans hugely affected the flow of tourism when the route through former Yugoslavia was cut off. It became impossible for many tourists to come to Greece by car, as they had done for many years, usually in July and August.

The season begins at Easter and lasts until early October, when the locals take their much-deserved vacation. Winter is the time for repairing old houses and building new ones. You can see the effects of urbanization when you compare Martha's pictures from the 1950s and 1960s with the present-day scene. The houses used to be small, with a garden for vegetables, vines and apple trees. Today most of the old houses have been pulled down and two- or three-storied ones put up. The upper floor is usually rented out to tourists and pilgrims.

It is all a bit of a disappointment. Most of the houses have the same architecture: they fill the entire garden. This results in narrow streets and an almost non-existent circulation of air during the hot season. A haze of traffic pollution covers Ouranoupolis, too. Asphalt streets have brought lorries and huge air-conditioned tourist buses. The smell of diesel is everywhere. Athens and Thessalonica should have been warning examples, but people never learn. Short-sighted self-interest goes before public welfare.

Hand-crafted windows give the finishing touch to the houses. It requires skill and flexibility to make the pieces fit. You would think that this philosophy was shared by the architects, but as elsewhere, the planners neither build the houses nor live in them. There seems to be a total lack of interaction. Once the windows have been fitted, the house is habitable. It is only the following winter, or even later, that the outside is finished.

Perhaps I am too critical, but I cannot stand by in silence. The wine may have loosened my tongue. I sincerely hope that my friends here will learn their lesson before it is too late. Some of the lorries from Athos are now forced to go via Tripiti, the first step in the right direction, I would say.

Every afternoon at around two o'clock, ships full of tourists dock at the jetty. The shop and *taverna*-keepers rub their hands in glee. The main street is soon crowded with potential buyers. Chefs advertise the superiority of their dishes in many languages. Manolis with his wheelbarrow taxi is in demand too: it is a busy time for the locals. Everyone has his own hunting ground, which is respected by others.

The only art shop, Akroathos, is different. Art is a way of life for its owner, Antonios. Making a profit is not the main aim in his life. It only provides the means to live a spiritual existence through art. This is why all of the artifacts and icons are connected with the spiritual struggle and history of the Holy Mountain.

The peaceful atmosphere in Akroathos makes Athonites feel at home. Many a discussion has taken place in the shop: confessions and spiritual guidance. It all helps the shopkeeper to keep faith in his humble way of life and to avoid being polluted by the urgency and superficiality of the tourists.

By comparison, the mealtimes at the *tavernas* are chaotic. I have to confess that I enjoy eating out at times, but I try hard not to take make it a habit. Ouranoupolis by night does not differ from any other village: light-hearted and joyful in the evening, downhearted and rueful next morning. As always! These two lifestyles, the spiritual life in accordance with the ancient Athonite Orthodoxy and the tourist business maximizing profit, are easily distinguishable by their differences: white is not white unless there is black, and grey cannot exist without contrasts. An anthropologist should be familiar with all aspects of human life, so I surrender to both.

3

LIFE IN OURANOUPOLIS ALWAYS SEEMS to pass in slow motion during the first two days of my sojourn. The atmosphere resembles that in silent films. From my seaside balcony the promenade is full of spasmodic movements: a lonely pilgrim headed for the jetty, local elderly women greeting each other in the morning sun, a truck emptying the garbage cans appears from the right and leaves the scene from the left. I am merely a member of the audience. Time passes slowly. Although I am quite familiar with the place after so many years, it still feels unreal not to have a hectic schedule. I have all the time I need, but what am I to do with it?

The pace seems painfully slow. It is ironic. First I want to get away and spend some quality time with myself and then, when it happens, I feel lost. So I almost immediately adopt a routine, or rather, the routine adopts me. After my morning tea with honey I go for a brisk walk, as if I were going to my office. Although my body is in Ouranoupolis, my spirit is still in Helsinki. I keep criss-crossing the village like a dog, sniffing for changes since last year, greeting old friends, wandering restlessly along the narrow streets, just for the fun of walking without any destination. Somehow it seems good to walk around after six hours in the air, the change of flight, the wait in the airport and the almost three-hour bus ride from Thessalonica to my Shangri-la, Ouranoupolis. I could, of course, equally well be having my morning tea in the *taverna*, reading the newspapers for hours, carrying on discussions with shopkeepers and passing friends, as I tend to do after a few days. After my restless tour of Ouranoupolis, I return to my balcony to embark on my spiritual journey by jotting down my thoughts in my diary, reflections that stem from the subconscious.

Flying is not a good way to travel. The spirit does not adjust as quickly to the new environment as the body does. In the last few years I have noticed that not even my body adjusts as quickly as it used to. Autumn is still much warmer in Greece than in Finland. It takes about three days to settle down physically and mentally. You cannot hasten the process. It is better to submit to it.

Reluctantly, I have learned to accept the fact that it takes time to get used to the rhythm of life in the village. It may have something to do with my getting older. Be that as it may, it is wiser to adjust gradually to the new tempo than stubbornly to follow a pre-programmed schedule. Adaptation, like creativity, follows its own course.

Ouranoupolis is truly a hesychastic village at this time of the year. However, the quiet does not mean total silence. Far from it. As I write these lines in my diary, my way of getting rooted into the present, I hear the caressing lapping of the waves on the shore as soon as I lift my pen and allow myself to enjoy the sounds of silence.

While seizing the day and my much-neglected inner self, I hear the soughing of the wind foreshadowing the winter ahead. It is a mighty breath that brings to mind the time when the spirit of God hovered over the surface of the water saying: "Let there be light!" There was light, and since then every morning reminds us of the creation of the first day at the beginning of time. The sage who observed that "the early bird catches the worm" also had a point. My worm is spiritual food for thought, or as Socrates might have said, reflection!

The peaceful morning is suddenly interrupted by elderly mothers shouting "*éla, éla*" in a high-pitched falsetto to hasten their children who are late for the school bus, shouts that echo in the narrow streets like the crackling voice of an old loudspeaker. "Come on, come on," they shriek in Greek, as the volume increases to a level that scares even the pigeons and makes the swallows fly away, only to return as soon as the bus has left the village.

Manolis, the village fool who is in his fifties, usually wakes up at the signal of the departing bus. He is the one with a grey wheelbarrow, on both sides of which he has painted *TAXI* in white letters. The daily newspapers arrive with the noon bus, and he has taken on the job of bringing the packages from the terminus to the news agent's shop.

Manolis is present whenever something is happening in the village. Even if he is not within sight, I have learned over the years to recognize his whereabouts by the noise of his shuffling as he drags his left foot behind him, lifting only his right one as he walks. The locals give him a *euro* or two for his help, and sometimes out of charity. Occasionally the younger men tease him until he loses his temper, something they do for lack of any better occupation. Eventually they make their peace with him, but not long before they know that he cannot take much more before becoming completely enraged. The first time I witnessed this mocking I felt awful, but now I have learned that it is a game that Manolis also enjoys to some extent. He likes to be at the center of attention, a celebrity if you like, though not in the usual sense of the word. Today he seems to be in a good mood. I can see this from my balcony as he waits for the bus by the tower.

My ears are so used to the noise of crowds and city traffic that the first days in the village always feel amazingly quiet, except for the incidents mentioned. I feel some relief, especially now that I am not going to the Holy Mountain for my field work. I am completely at ease as I look out on the open sea. The aim of this sojourn is different. I desperately want to find the monastic island I came across unexpectedly in a book in Helsinki University Library as I was checking some travellers' accounts of the Holy Mountain. It has become a habit of mine to make a sort of academic odyssey in search of interesting books in the late afternoons when there is no energy left for serious work. It is better to take a creative break every now and then than to force yourself to struggle on. In my everyday life I follow the philosophy of the Ant rather than that of the Grasshopper, but the older I get the more convinced I become that the idle Grasshopper also has a valid point. To work and work and work and work cannot be the sole purpose of life. There are also other values, and at my age I have already dragged quite a few bales of straw to the heap. I deserve a break. Call me the rebellious Ant for all I care. Being here in Ouranoupolis is my bonus to myself, and I feel no guilt about it.

The library is the world's greatest treasure trove. There you find answers to all your questions and an insight into what human-kind has been pondered on from the very beginning of civiliza-tion. Oddly enough, I learned this years ago from a carpenter. When, as a child, I asked him what he was looking for in his tool box, he answered enigmatically: "I don't know!" For a long time I watched him patiently grubbing in the box, his fingers quickly putting nails, screws, and tools aside while digging deeper down to the bottom. Suddenly he exclaimed: "Here's a piece of rub-ber I can use as a washer between the moving parts to prevent rubbing." There was no spare part to be found in the shop so the carpenter had to invent one. He had confidently searched for something to replace the broken part without exactly know-ing what he was looking for. The important thing was that he regarded the problem as one that could be solved. When you know why you are looking for a solution, it usually reveals itself if only you have faith in the possibility.

I often think about this as I browse through the shelves in the library, allowing the names of the books and their enticing covers to seduce me momentarily like the alluring songs of the sirens, until the cover of some other volume catches my eye. Odysseus and his cunning taught me to tame my imagination by tying it tightly to discernment, which I use to distinguish unique opportunities from enticing temptations. In life you need to know when to seize a golden opportunity and when to ignore passing trivia. These days this kind of insight is an indispensable asset. Computers spit out printed matter and books at an ever-increasing rate and it is no longer possible to read everything *tutti quanti.* Too many people waste their valuable time reading trashy literature without ever encountering the pearls mankind has concealed between lines of eloquence and discernment. I have to admit, though, that even lightweight novels may contain the odd thought that stimulates the reader to move on in his or her thinking.

It was on one such odyssey in the library that I happened to find a lithograph of a monastic island in the Greek archipelago, made by the Venetian mathematician and cosmographer Vincenzo Coronelli (d. 1718) and printed in 1688. It was love at first sight. I was struck by a compelling desire to visit that island. I decided straightaway to go there at any price. "This is the chance of a lifetime," I thought, "and I will not miss it for anything in the world." Deep inside I was totally convinced that visiting the island would be the turning point in my life that I had long been waiting for. I knew that my destiny was sealed on that island. Strangely enough, I was also convinced that the island really existed, and that Christos would know its whereabouts. After all, he was a fisherman.

The rays of the sun gradually warm my body, touching me gently as I have my tea and toast at my favorite *taverna*. Since childhood I have always put honey in my tea, never milk or sugar. "Tea with honey keeps me going" has been my motto for as long as I can remember.

My thoughts run wild like horses let out to pasture. On the second morning of my sojourn I never fail to enjoy listening to the silence and feeling the warmth of the autumn sun. From earlier visits I know that this table is the one that catches the first rays of the sun as they peep over the roof of the *taverna*. This is useful knowledge, as the mornings are getting chilly and I still want to welcome the dawn of the new day with both heart and soul.

"*Carpe diem!*" I urge myself. "Seize the moment. This is the turning point of my life. There is no room for compromise."

I was thrown into this world without my consent. In all probability, I will have to leave it equally unwillingly. The words of *Ecclesiastes* come to mind: "For everything its season, and for every activity under heaven its time: a time to be born and a time to die; a time to plant and a time to uproot; a time to kill and a time to heal; a time to break down and a time to build up; a time to weep and a time to laugh; a time for mourning and a time for dancing; a time to scatter stones and a time to gather them; a time to embrace and a time to abstain from embracing; a time to seek and a time to lose; a time to keep and a time to discard; a time to tear and a time to mend; a time for silence and a time for speech; a time to love and a time to hate; a time for war and a time for peace. What profit has the worker from his labor?"

The words saddened me at first, but then, to my delight, I remembered the response: "I know that there is nothing good for anyone except to be happy and live the best life he can while he is alive. Indeed, that everyone should eat and drink and enjoy himself, in return for all his labours, is a gift of God." So there is no reason for me to feel guilty about the duties left behind and the work undone. Now is not a time to weep, but a time to allow the spirit to dance, laugh and be merry.

I am a pilgrim in life. The beginning and the end are not in my control. This moment is, though. Whether to throw myself into the fleeting social whirl to counterbalance the stressful work, the rat race as it were, or to sit down on a bench for a while watching people rush by—that is my question. Every now and then the nagging feeling of being inefficient entices me like demonic sirens tempting me to jump into the main stream. It is only with great difficulty, and by listening attentively to the voice of my heart, that I have at times managed to avoid the trap. I have had the determination to stay ashore and to reflect upon what it means to become human through culture.

When I finished my tea it was only ten o'clock. I took a long walk alone along the winding seashore. The village houses seem to be spread along it like white pearls decorating the fringe of a blue sea. It is a beautiful sight. The contrast of white and blue is timelessly æsthetic. All the new houses are built in the same architectural style; on two floors with white quadrangles and narrow balconies with brown balustrades running around the house. Blue and white are everywhere, and I think I understand why the flag of Greece, like that of Finland, is blue and white. These colors dominate the country, so that even the tables and chairs in the traditional *tavernas* are blue and the tablecloths white.

Then, by the port at the end of the seashore, I see the imposing grey Byzantine tower with its massive walls rising on rocks from the sea—a shelter and a watch-tower! Unfortunately, the door has been closed all these years I have been passing through to the Holy Mountain. The Ouranoupolitans plan to turn it into a museum on Byzantium and the history of the village, but the restoration is proceeding slowly and I am not convinced that the work will be finished during my lifetime. I have not been able to climb the steps to the top of the tower and look at the sights from its wooden balcony, as I am certain thousands have done before me. The wooden structure was found to be too brittle after the death of Mrs. Joice Loch. It was no longer safe to climb the four flights, and the place was locked up. I have climbed many towers on the Holy Mountain, however, and it is not difficult for me to imagine how the monks in the medieval days kept watch for pirates as they enjoyed the sunset and listened to the waves lapping around the rocks on the seashore.

Perhaps it is just as well that the door is closed. What I need is not merely to enjoy the beautiful scenery, but rather to sojourn on the monastic island and clarify my inner thoughts, which tend to surface spontaneously in this evocative atmosphere of quiet and stillness. Ouranoupolis provides me with convenient shelter against the winds of worldliness: the hypersensitive Protestant sense of duty and responsibility, the distracting and trivial habits of collecting and buying books, reading magazines, listening to the radio and my CDs, watching television, window-shopping, going to parties and other social gatherings, and taking part in so-called important and urgent meetings, erudite academic seminars and roundtable discussions: all of these things, like pirates, rob me of my biggest treasure—time!

In my thoughts I am sitting on the balcony gazing at where the blue sea meets the sky. The sun's rays glittering on the sea stir me to reflect upon the human conditions on earth. Thoughts bubble up from my subconscious to the surface of my awareness.

Time is certainly the most precious gift we are given. It equals lifetime. Every day gnaws at our stock of it, and by evening there is a little less sand in our hourglass. It is not insignificant how we spend our days. In my youth, people still had hobbies. They talked about them with the enthusiasm and innocence of children. Adults had hobbies as such—not merely to counterbalance a hectic life, but as a source of inspiration, meaning and inner tranquility.

Nowadays few speak about their hobbies in this carefree tone, notably only retired people. Expressions like "active holiday," "quality time," "counterbalance," "work hard, play hard" and "maintaining working capacity" reveal that people have lost their ability to enjoy free time without losing their sense of guilt and the drive to be efficient. They appear to have a distorted sense of duty. It harasses them and whispers in their ears like the devil viper by the tree of knowledge of good and evil in the garden of Eden: "I really shouldn't go on vacation. I still have too much unfinished work on my desk," or "I have to finish this job before I can go on vacation."

Many people always have work on their mind. Only a few appear to have learned the lesson taught by the essayist Michel de Montaigne (d. 1592): "Leave your daily worries at your office as you go home!" There is always a tomorrow, and even if for some reason that were not the case, there will be someone else who is eager to finish the job and get all the credit for it. No matter how hard you work, there is no end to it. Workaholism is as damaging as any other addiction.

Reading the obituaries in the daily newspapers after lunch is an obsession of mine. It is highly educational both culturally and regarding the life history of the prominent person who has passed away. The columns are rewarding in that they usually provide information about the deceased's career and philosophy of life. The saddest ones are the superlative-laden ones of middle-aged men. They praise his work ethic, the way he treated his colleagues and his sense of duty and responsibility. These are important, there is no denying that, but the old saying, "Heroes die young, wise men live to old age," gives cause for reflection and the re-evaluation of our priorities. Too many bright, attentive and focused men have died prematurely. The praise in the obituary is all too fleeting in comparison with a long life lived to its full.

Ouranoupolis offers me an excellent haven against the kind of excessive work that has become the disease of our time. Here my innate inclination towards sweet idleness or, in the Italian expression, *il dolce far niente*, accompanied by the ideal conditions, first loosens the Protestant hold on me and then teaches me moderation. Moderation is the word in Ouranoupolis. When I have my afternoon coffee, I have it *métrio*, which means with just one spoon of sugar. I similarly ration my wine, food, exercise, work—everything. The Athonites speak about *engráteia* when they mean "sobriety," "restraint" and "abstinence." Suddenly I am totally clear in my mind as to what is essential in life, what trivial. My way of life, like that of so many other people, has its roots in an internalized sense of duty and responsibility, which have never been seriously questioned. This is quite dangerous to those who identify themselves with their work and consider themselves irreplaceable. Nobody is indispensable, as I have learned the hard way.

In difficult times I often come to think about my grandmother, who lived her life in harmony with the words of wisdom concealed in aphorisms and poems. Her attitude towards life and its trials was romantic and nostalgic in an optimistic way. She knew quite a few maxims and poems by heart, and turned to them in her hours of need, especially during her last days. She died peacefully, reminding herself how fleeting life is. She never had any material wealth, but out of her inner wealth I profited from many a wise word during my childhood. The poem by Johan Olof Wallin (d. 1839) on the "Value of Time," which she often recited to me, is timeless and excellent food for thought.

Money you may lose,
Money still regain,
A casket you may choose,
Your treasure to retain.
But time spent,
Heaven sent,
You can never take again.

These lines were also recalled by a late professor of mine. After a long illness, when on his deathbed, he said to me: "I don't know anyone, who, lying here, has regretted that he didn't spend more time at the department."

As we have only a limited number of days in our lives, over the years I have become more and more choosy about how I spend them. I am no longer willing to give up my quality time, in other words the moments I spontaneously feel I am completely alive, like a puppy who, happy and unconcerned about tomorrow, plays around on the lawn. Quality time has no time, no yesterday and no tomorrow. Only the present matters. Time is now! Time spent wisely is life lived to the full. This is the best consolation when the end is near, when we are forced to balance our accounts. This is well expressed in the aphorism: "Death lies heavily on the shoulders of someone who passes away known to everyone, but unknown to himself." Obituaries frequently prove this to be true. Perhaps this was also the wisdom hidden in the saying of the ancient Greeks, who urge us: "Know thyself."

4

ROM AFAR THE BYZANTINE TOWER truly resembles an exclamation mark, warning me to watch out for my inclinations towards materialism and vanity. With its silent and majestic appearance, accompanied by the breath of a soft autumn wind, it whispers the eternal truth: *Festina lente; memento mori!* (Make haste slowly; Remember that you are mortal!)

The tower has become a living symbol for me. It reminds me that every now and again it is advisable to withdraw to a convenient niche that provides solitude, stillness and spiritual struggle. With age I have become increasingly in need of spending time with myself, discussing with myself and thus learning more about myself. I want to understand the movements of my body and my soul, to listen to my inner thoughts, and to learn to navigate the storms of life and to find a balance. I want to be like a skillful sailor who knows when to tighten the ropes and when to slacken them, when to hoist the sails and when to haul them down, when to find a safe haven from the wind and when to recharge the batteries, lolling about with friends and enjoying good wine. The Mediterranean people learned this skill ages ago.

The Ouranoupolis cove and the monasteries on the Holy Mountain have been my spiritual haven on more than twenty occasions. At the first opportunity, I have withdrawn here to detach myself from the drudgery of everyday life at the university. Intoxicated by the demands of administration, I easily lose my sense of balanced judgement. Irritation tends to build its nest in my temper. Fighting for money and prestige as well as for the future of my post-graduates drains my energy. Then, when my writing does not flow as it should, I usually realize that I have ignored my inner life for far too long.

Life seems meaningless. When that feeling surfaces in my mind, I know it is time to leave for Ouranoupolis. It is no use running if the road in front of you is long. Whatever work we are doing, it is useful to stop for a while and reassess our priorities. This enables us to see more clearly not only what we are doing at the time, but also what it all means in the long run, in the wider perspective of our lifespan. It puts things in proportion.

As these thoughts are crossing my mind I suddenly see a man with a long wooden pilgrim's stick. At first he appears only in profile, but as I watch him intently I am mightily surprised to recognise myself. I am that pilgrim. I am the homeless nomad, the seeker, born to wander. "Where are you going?" I ask him. The mysterious figure does not answer me. He simply looks elsewhere and goes away.

At that very moment, the heat of the sun woke me up on the beach. Quickly I looked around, but I realized that it was only a dream. Falling asleep in the sun is dangerous, so I immediately went for a swim. This is the disadvantage of being alone. There is nobody to keep you awake. The manly figure continued to bother my mind even after the swim. I could not avoid thinking about him. "Who am I?" I was anxious to find an answer to that question.

In my thoughts, I climbed the tower and stood on the uppermost balcony looking in all directions, and the waves reflected images from my past. Since my early youth I have felt estranged from the mentality, attitudes and values of the Finns. I sing my songs in Swedish, the second official language of Finland. I have never felt like a Finn in my heart. For some inconceivable reason I have always been an outsider. I was born a Finland-Swede, but even that I have found hard to totally identify with. At times I have longed for a sense of belonging, but on the whole I have enjoyed being on the margin.

In my outsider status I am like a Jew, who is a foreigner in all countries except Israel, without a homeland on earth. This has been my blessing in many ways. From my youth I have felt as if I were under the auspices of a guardian angel, sent to me by our heavenly Father. I cannot explain this in rational terms. This is just how it is. My days, like everyone's, are numbered, but in a childish way I trust that the tasks given to me in this life will be accomplished. Therefore I try not to worry about it.

There are two kinds of people, those who build a nest and those who are pilgrims in their heart of hearts. The nest-builders are down-to-earth people. For them the land, language and nationality is of major importance. Pilgrims are different, and although they might own land, in their hearts they identify with the Biblical view of life as a pilgrimage on earth. For them the meaning of life is in making the inner journey and in making progress along the spiritual path rather than in becoming rooted in a particular place or society. Why this is so I do not know, and it does not matter to me. What I find much more relevant is the fact that for many years I have conceived of myself as an unknown pilgrim. Although I sometimes curse my fate under the false impression that life would be easier if I could whole-heartedly identify with the nest-builders, I would never be prepared to give up the wanderer's freedom. In this I follow the advice of the great Roman poet Horace (d. 8 BC), who stated, "[I am] not bound to swear allegiance to my masters, wherever the wind takes me I travel as a visitor" (*Epistles*, Book. I, no 1. 1.14).

Some years ago I read a book in which the energy of creativity was characterized as a state of flow. All artists and writers are familiar with the feeling of slumbering energy that begins to stream creatively, as if spontaneously. Sometimes they cannot stop the flow and are burned out in the process. Usually though, the energy dries up by itself. To experience the flow of inspiration is such a delight and joy that the sacrifices made and sufferings undergone are trivial in comparison.

I had my first experience of the creative flow when I was sixteen. Like so many other teenagers in the 1960s, I played the guitar and wrote songs of my own. Naturally they were love songs—what else could one expect of a teenager in love? I still recall a September morning in the mid-60s when, to my own surprise, a song with words and a tune came into my mind as if from nowhere and I merely took it all in *tutti quanti*. I was only the humble medium of some higher power. Since then I have always tried to listen to my inner voice. I became convinced of the existence of a creative energy, an intuition, like the helm in a sailing boat. I have never had cause to regret it when I have followed the direction pointed out by that energy. On the contrary, when I have ignored it, things have turned out wrong and there have been many recriminations. Even now, mid-life, I occasionally hum my love song, and whenever it comes to mind I feel alive and warmth envelops my heart.

> You have been so good to me,
> The only one I love to see,
> You are the sweetest thing
> I've seen since the day that I was born.
>
> You made me happy when
> You came into my life again,
> You are the sweetest thing
> I've seen since the day that I was born.
>
> You made the sun
> You made it all
> A place to live
> For everyone
> You paved my way
> That very day
> I am so thankful Mr. Grey
> You've been my one true friend
> There for me until the end
> You are the sweetest thing
> I've seen since the day that I was born.

The waves reflect more images from my past. The spiritual threads of my life are suddenly discernible in the midst of the everyday greyness. Having finally finished secondary school I found myself face to face with difficult and momentous decision. What was I to do now?

Only two decisions in life are of real importance: the choice of education, in other words of career, and the choice of a life partner. If you are successful in these, the grande finale of life, the attitude to adapt to the process of dying and death will also be bearable. At least this is what I believe and hope.

At first I had no idea what to study. There were too many options. I felt, as most elderly people always tend to say, that I had the whole world ahead of me. Finally, when the application deadlines for the various departments at the university were given in the newspapers, I sat down on my yoga mat in full lotus position—oh yes, I regularly practised yoga at that time—and carefully considered all the professions I was absolutely sure I would not enjoy in the long run. Having thus eliminated the unthinkable options, there were only a few choices left. I trusted my intuition, my discernment, which previous experience told me I could count on.

Consequently, I applied to the Department of Theology at the University of Helsinki, not for religious reasons in the ordinary sense, but because I had the persistent feeling that a life without reflecting on the meaning of life was not worth living—to paraphrase Socrates (*Apologia* 38a)—and that if I could find the meaning of my own life or make my everyday life appear meaningful to me, everything else would turn out right in the end. Moreover, I knew that the Department of Theology would provide me with the broadest possible education. Apart from Latin, Hebrew and Biblical Greek, I would have to study exegesis, church history, dogmatics, ethics, the history of religions, philosophy, psychology, sociology, social anthropology, and of course practical theology. Very few people know that theological studies in Finland cover such a broad spectrum of subjects. During the whole process of evaluating my educational options I never once thought about how much I would earn if I were to study this or that subject. My choice and decision were purely philosophical. I have never regretted it.

Some years ago, one of the communist leaders in Finland astonished nearly all of his party members, and the public for that matter, by stating that the best education he ever received was in the Department of Theology. He was able to study atheism critically, too. I should perhaps explain that he was originally a left-wing priest who eventually became a full-time politician. When he made that statement he was attacked by some of his party members for being a priest—and the above statement was his response.

This statement still holds true today, and I believe it is the same in many other countries. Non-theologians always tend to belittle the education of theologians, which I know to be the best you can possibly get if you are interested in the art and meaning of human life. I could, of course, have studied philosophy, but somehow I was even then convinced that theology provided a much broader education, and this is still the case. With hindsight, I now understand that, for me, there was no other way. If the key to a harmonious life was not be found in theology, it would not be found at all.

Ouranoupolis is my belvedere. Here I can rest my eyes on the eternal waves of the Aegean Sea, listen to the voices of my inner self and wait for the ideas to flow. How can I achieve a balance between my selfish ambitions and my sense of altruistic obedience to what makes man human and humble, and what makes God "God?" After all, it seems to me that we are all here for some greater purpose than merely swimming in the tide of the latest trends.

Some people are aware that the tower in Ouranoupolis has, since ancient times, been the last point at the neck of the Athonite peninsula to which women can go. All men know for certain that man can resist the temptations of lust and pleasure only with difficulty. Thus, this little village, deserted by the tourists for the winter, is a natural place to withdraw to for a period of reflection in the spirit of Socrates and the holy fathers, there being one temptress less to watch out for.

Pilgrimage by the Book

I

I WAS EXHAUSTED, SO I WENT TO bed early. The change of
climate and the hectic previous week had used up the last
of my energy. Before travelling I had just finished my entry
on pilgrimage and posted it from the airport to Dr. Peter Jones,
who is editing an encyclopedia of religion.

As I have learned from experience, unfinished work usually
bothers the mind. No wonder I felt an incredible sense of relief
when I let the envelope fall into the letter box. My Protestant
conscientiousness was satisfied. Now I had the right to relax and
enjoy my holiday. My diligence and sense of responsibility were
rewarded. I deserved my few weeks off, though the word "deserved"
sounds a bit strange. Sometimes I have found it almost impossible
to throw myself into sweet idleness, as if I have lost the capability
of merely being in the world.

It is very laborious to write entries for encyclopedias. You have
to compress the information into a limited number of words and
write clearly so that the ordinary reader will understand the subject correctly. Verbs are, of course, the cornerstones of sentences.
They describe the action, the condition and the experience.

The preamble to an entry should comprise the core of the subject. Eventually I ended up with the following introduction.

> Pilgrimage as a phenomenon is to be found in all
> world religions, i.e. Hinduism, Buddhism, Judaism,
> Christianity and Islam, but also in the Chinese,
> Japanese and other ethnic religious traditions. It is
> a form of devotion, sometimes even an ascetic reli-
> gious exercise. The traveller is headed for a place
> or religious center considered to be sacred. The

tombs of martyrs and saints as well as their living quarters and places of sojourn were the first sacred centers of pilgrimage. The original motive for visiting these places was to honor the memory of the martyrs, but the earliest pilgrims also wished to share in the spiritual virtues of the religious *virtuosi*. Unusual rocks and mountains, inhabited by ascetics and spiritual strivers who practiced severe asceticism in caves and huts built by themselves, also attracted pilgrims from the very beginning of the ascetic movement. In time, these hermitages were turned into large monasteries, which today are popular centers of pilgrimage not only for their relics and icons, but also for their miracles.

We who are born into the Judeo-Christian tradition tend to ask ourselves what the origin of the word "pilgrimage" is. Therefore, the introduction of every entry on this subject carries a brief paragraph on the concept of "pilgrimage." Dr. Jones certainly expected me to start by defining the word. Consequently, I began by explaining that the English word "pilgrim" comes from the Latin *peregrinus*, which principally refers to one who is walking in an alien land; from *peregre* "abroad," from *perger* "being abroad," from *per* "through" and *ager* "land," "field." Originally, *peregrinus* meant a foreigner who lived outside the territory of Rome and travelled or walked around. It was synonymous with traveller in the sense of wayfarer, someone who passes through life as if in exile from a heavenly homeland, or in search of some higher goal, such as truth. A pilgrimage, then, simply means the "journey of a pilgrim," especially a journey to a shrine or sacred place. Its wider meaning is the course of life on earth.

The journey to Jerusalem was long and demanding, hence the connotation of travelling through fields. The Greek word for pilgrim, *proskynitís* meaning "worshipper," from the verb *proskynó*, "to fall down and worship," "to do obeisance to the gods or their images," "to avert divine wrath," has an entirely different connotation, however. Greeks go to shrines and sacred places to kiss the icons, to venerate the relics, to make confession, to discuss personal matters with their spiritual fathers and, above all, to take part in Holy Communion. Since shrines were everywhere, the Greeks never had much interest in travelling to Jerusalem. Therefore a pilgrimage in the Greek context, to the Holy Mountain of Athos for example, is not necessarily a journey in the *peregrinus* sense, but a resting in the monastery and a taking part in the Divine Liturgy, the celebration of Holy Communion being its spiritual climax.

From the lexical meanings we know that *peregrinus* refers to one who is walking (in an alien land), whereas *proskynitís* denotes one who kneels down in front of an icon or the *proskynitárion*, for example. When the connotations of these two words are compared, it becomes clear that *peregrinus* is more closely connected with the New Testament and the practice of identifying oneself with Christ, re-enacting his Passion and thereby purifying oneself: that is, the theology of *imitatio Christi*. *Proskynitís*, on the other hand, is more closely connected with the Old Testament and the reliving of the Fall, with the recitation of "*Kyrie, eleison*" ("Lord, have mercy on me, a sinner") as the manifest sign of the renewed relationship between Lord and humble servant.

In the conclusion of my entry I wrote:

> The concept of 'pilgrimage' has two opposite meanings: wandering and resting. This is not immediately obvious in the English word, but in Finland, for example, the Lutherans and the Roman Catholics talk about pilgrimage (Fin. *pyhiinvaellus*) as travelling or wandering, while the Orthodox use the expression "visiting the Holy" (Fin. *pyhissäkäyminen*). In the Western tradition, pilgrimage is regarded more as an activity, a travelling, and a identification with the sufferings of Christ by means of ascetic wandering and praying. For the Orthodox it is the cry of the humble servant for Christ's mercy (*Kyrie, eleison*) that is the motive for going to the Holy place. There are two different paths to the same goal. Our religious tradition and

personality dictate which path each one of us will choose.

On one of my odysseys in the library I came across an article in which Professor Markus, a specialist on the history of early Christianity, poses the question: "How on earth could places become holy?" He discusses the origins of the Christian idea of holy places. Because the center of any pilgrimage is conceived of as a holy and sacred place, I read with great interest what the most recent research had to say about the matter. I then added some paragraphs about the earliest history of the holy places in Christianity to my own encyclopedic entry.

Apparently the early Christians did not attribute holiness to places. There is no evidence that Jewish Christians or other Christians designated sites as holy or sacred before the beginning of the fourth century. Their attitude towards holy places and pilgrimage was, in fact, negative.

Eusebius of Caesarea (d. 339), for example, was extremely reluctant to countenance any talk of holy places. Moses had promised a holy land to the Jews. Holy places were what Jews and pagans had. Christianity, in contrast, was a spiritual religion, and Jesus had promised his followers a "much greater land, truly holy and beloved of God, not located in Judea." Only a heavenly Jerusalem could be the holy city for the Christians. Pilgrimage was prescribed neither in the Bible nor by the Church Fathers.

Fifty years later, Cyril of Jerusalem (d. 386) was the first bishop to embrace Emperor Constantine's enthusiasm for building churches on biblical sites in Jerusalem, which he did after the Council of Nicæa in 325. "Others merely hear," Cyril argued to his catechumens, "we see and touch." Historical curiosity combined with pious zeal began to motivate an ever-increasing number of converts to go and see the biblical sites where Jesus was born, lived his earthly life, and was crucified and resurrected.

To Cyril, Jerusalem was a holy city not because God had been involved there in the past, but because it had "a specific quality in the present." The ritual processions around the churches and the related sites replaced the prevailing pagan, Jewish and Samaritan cults in places that had a biblical association. This brought the physical sites and the narrating of the corresponding biblical events into close proximity. In Jerusalem, story, liturgy, and site became one. The past became the present.

Until the end of the fourth century, then, Jerusalem as a holy city evoked mixed feelings. Gregory of Nyssa (d. 394) considered it necessary to excuse his visit there by stating that travelling to Jerusalem did not bring man closer to God. The early Christians did not consider their churches as temples of a divinity. They were built solely for the specific purpose of congregating and gathering "the living temples" of God—the Christians—into one. It was the gathered community and their liturgy that were holy, not the church that housed them nor the place per se.

Attitudes towards relics were also ambivalent at first. Vigilantius (born 370) criticized the Christians by arguing that their means of honoring God were similar to those used previously to honor pagan gods, and that martyrs were now honored in ways that were previously considered idolatrous. The decisive and final shift in attitude corresponded to Augustine's (d. 430) own acceptance of the prevalent belief in the everyday occurrence of miracles, which arose in the two first decades of the fifth century. His change in attitude was brought about when, almost daily in his pastoral work among his congregations, he witnessed miracles wrought by the relics of St. Stephen, which had recently been discovered and brought to Africa.

In her account (c. 381-84) of the then popular habit of visiting *martyria*, or churches that had been built on the tomb of a martyr or saint, the pilgrim Egeria remarked that specific passages from scripture had become attached to specific sites and the events associated with them. She also noted that the monks in the region of Charra of Mesopotamia lived in seclusion and came out only occasionally, notably at Easter and for the feast of the martyr.

It seems that the cult of martyrs prepared the way for the idea of holy places, and in fact gave the place a new sacred significance: it linked the Church of the present to the persecuted Church of the past. It also abolished the gap between the generation of martyrs and later generations. The places were derivatively rather than intrinsically holy, but they were the sites of historical events of sacred significance. The miracles witnessed in the *martyria* in particular were the cause of the rapid growth of the pilgrimage movement in the early fifth century. Images became popular, too, as a result of miracle-working icons.

Hence Professor Markus concluded that since it was not the place but the congregation and the relics that were originally regarded as holy in the early Eastern Churches, visitors or pilgrims did not need to make the journey to the temple or to the "holy places" of Christendom. To them, pilgrimage implied spiritual participation in the life of Christ, as expressed in the liturgy. This attitude gave rise to another kind of pilgrimage, namely that of visiting holy men and women who had dedicated their lives to perpetual prayer: monks and ascetics. The early Christians understood the words of St. Paul literally: "The God who created the world and everything in it, and who is Lord of heaven and earth, does not live in shrines made by human hands" (Acts 17:24). Moreover, they referred to the words of God: "And the temple of the living God is what we are" (2 Cor. 6:16).

When Basil of Caesarea (d. 379) visited Palestine in 351, he stayed there with the monks and ascetics in order to unlock the secret of their holy lives. He wanted to learn about personal spiritual pilgrimage. The destination was not Jerusalem, but the heavenly city of God as internally experienced.

With the growth of the ascetic movement, the monasteries and hermitages in fourth-century Egypt soon gave it the status of a second Holy Land. Travellers who visited Jerusalem also felt an urgent need to visit the ascetic houses of the Nile. Most monasteries became pilgrimage centers in the following centuries, notably St. Catherine's on Mount Sinai, built in the sixth century on the site of the Burning Bush at the foot of the craggy peak where God delivered the Tablets to Moses, and the great monastery of Studios in Constantinople. This development went hand-in-hand with the cults of relics and images, and with the veneration of holy men and women. All newly founded monasteries had some relics, which also became objects of veneration on the death of well-known hermits and spiritual fathers.

2

To BRING A COMPARATIVE ASPECT to my entry, I used a search program and typed in the keyword "pilgrimage." The printer churned out a long list of articles and books. I did not count the number of references, but there were certainly several hundred bibliographical notes. Although I narrowed it down to theories, the number of references was still huge. I began to suspect that pilgrimage may well become one of the most popular religious phenomena during the first decade of the new millennium. Santiago de Compostela in particular seems to be on everyone's lips. This convinced me that I needed to add a few paragraphs on the various theories of pilgrimage.

I began with Victor Turner's (d. 1983) theory as a starting point of my research. It is the one most referred to, though also the most criticized. I suggested in my review that his interest in pilgrimage was more theoretical than ethnographic. It was guided primarily by his pretentious eagerness to produce a comparative study of ritual symbols and social processes. The model, built up principally from the statements of officiants, is based on two propositions: (1) pilgrimage is a process of moving from the familiar (or structural) to the anti-structural "other" and back, and (2) the period of being away from structure, the *liminal* period, is characterized by the existence of a *communitas* mood of relationship among participants.

Regarding the first proposition, I agreed with him that pilgrimage forms an ellipse. Pilgrims may return by the way they came, yet ellipse is the apt metaphor for the total journey, because "the return road is, psychologically, different from the approach road." This ellipse metaphor is acclaimed by many other scholars. According to Alan Morinis, for example, "Every instance of pilgrimage must have a journey from home to sacred center and return to home." Although this is, of course, an inevitable condition of any travel, it is not such a trivial observation after all, as I will point out later on.

When Turner shifted his attention from African tribal societies and the study of mid-transition in transition rites in particular to the phenomenon of pilgrimage, he was naturally struck by the similarity in the sequence structure between the two. Pilgrimages, he asserts, have attributes both of the wider community, the "earth shrine," types of ritual we have glanced at in Africa, and of the *liminal* stage of transition rites. Thus—as Morinis perceptively remarked—he transposed the model developed in the African tribal context, in other words the concepts of *liminality* and *communitas*, onto his pilgrimage material, which contained data principally from Roman Catholic Mexico, spiced with a few selective examples from Hinduism, Buddhism and Islam.

According to Turner, pilgrimages have the following attributes of *liminality* in their transition rites: temporary release from the mundane structure that normally binds; release from the burdens of stress, anxiety and guilt; movement from the mundane center to a sacred periphery; homogenization of status; simplicity of dress and behavior; reflection on the meaning of basic religious and cultural values; the ritualized enactment of correspondence between religious paradigms and shared human experience; and experience of human brotherhood and sisterhood.

In a recent study on Arnold van Gennep, Lévy Zumwalt eloquently brought into focus the difference between Turner's interpretation of the *liminal* stage and van Gennep's notion of the marginal state, *rites de marge,* in the theory of *rites de passage.* Turner conceived the *liminal* phase as outside the ordered universe, a period betwixt and between the categories of ordinary social life, while van Gennep, strictly speaking, intended *liminal* rites to denote the transition from one social status to another. His focus was on the patterned relationship *between* the stages and not on the lack of order *during* the *liminal* period. The interpretation of "during a *liminal* period" is Turner's and not van Gennep's.

Van Gennep used the concept "passage" to denote a transition rite in which there is (1) a shift of social status, (2) coinciding with a life-cycle transition such as birth, social puberty (sexuality), initiation to various age groups, admission to a monastic institution or secret community, marriage, fatherhood/motherhood, social mobility, occupational specialization and death—more or less predetermined transitions which are (3) publicly confirmed. Moreover, the transition rite is (4) a one-way passage that is irreversible since there is no return, and because it is (5) inevitable, it is in that sense obligatory in every tribal society.

It is of course true that there is a similarity in sequence structure between a transition rite and a pilgrimage. However, Turner was deceived by this. Similarity in sequence structure does not necessarily mean that a pilgrimage is a transition rite, as he erroneously concluded. The differences in function and motive are fundamental. Whereas the function of the transition rite is to facilitate the transposition of the "passenger," or "*liminar*," to his new social status and to integrate him without violent social disruptions into society, the purpose of the pilgrimage is to facilitate detachment from mundane concerns and reunification between the pilgrim and God—Buddhism being an exception.

The attributes of a pilgrimage are, in fact, the opposite of those of a transition rite. In pilgrimage there is no publicly confirmed shift of social status that coincides with predetermined life-cycle transitions. Nor is there an irreversible one-way passage—there is a return! Moreover, a pilgrimage is not inevitable or obligatory. It is the spontaneous and voluntary choice of an individual pilgrim to travel, often incognito, to a terra incognita. The aspect of travelling anonymously is one of the essential meanings of "pilgrim." As already noted, a *peregrinus* was a foreigner who lived in an alien land outside the territory of Rome (*ager Romanus*) and who travelled around incognito.

I definitely disagree with Turner's second proposition. The specific quality of a pilgrimage is not the *communitas*, a Latin word he adopted to refer to the social relationship, fellowship and social bond, the spontaneously generated relationship between levelled and equal human beings on a collective and an individual level, stripped of structural attributes. *Communitas* constitutes a sort of anti-structure. Turner regards it as the *fons et origo* of all social structures and, at the same time, their critique. It represents a striving towards universalism and openness.

Turner argues that the *communitas* character of pilgrimage makes it democratic. The secular distinction of rank and status disappears or is homogenized. In this sense, pilgrimage presents a living model of human brotherhood and sisterhood. Pilgrims travel in fellowship: there is a strong tendency among them to develop an intense comradeship, and occasionally even life-long friendships. Pilgrims become like brothers and there is fellowship with the like-minded. *Communitas* is a concept used to denote cohesion in a group of pilgrims based on an immediate and total feeling of affinity, solidarity and togetherness. These lines of thought are nothing more than what Ferdinand Tönnies refers to with the concept *Gemeinschaft* ("community"). This includes "social structure" in the sense of bonds between members of tightly knit, multi-functional groups, usually with a local basis, friendship as expressing a kind of "feeling of affinity," in other words a *Gemeinschaft* that is tied to neither blood nor locality.

The hypothesis that these *communitas* moods are characteristic features of all pilgrimages has been incontrovertibly disproved by scholars who have field-tested it. Morinis, who reviewed all of the relevant empirical findings on the subject in his chapter on the theoretical perspectives of pilgrimages, explicitly points out that the quality of *communitas* that Turner considers an essential feature is *not universal*. Michael Sallnow (d. 1990), who studied sponsored group pilgrimages among Peruvian highland peasants, arrived at the same conclusion: "On the journey the various parties of pilgrims from different communities maintained a ritualized distance from one another which accentuated, rather than attenuated, the boundaries between them. At the shrine itself they each maintained their separateness, and never coalesced into a single unified congregation... the concept of *communitas* is of little value in explaining the essentially decisive quality of Andean pilgrimage... It would be more appropriate in such circumstances to see community, not *communitas*, as the hallmark of pilgrimage."

In my entry I therefore argued that to conceive of the pilgrimage process as a shift from the structural to the anti-structural and back is both reductionistic and irrelevant. It is reductionistic in that it reduces pilgrimage to the phenomenon of festal solidarity and *communitas*, although its significance lies beyond the movements of the pilgrims.

It is true that pilgrims occasionally experience a feeling of affinity among themselves, but they nevertheless maintain a distinctive social structure, as many scholars have pointed out. To use the Latin word *communitas* for that temporary feeling of affinity does not make the observation more scholarly. It is, in fact, beside the point and irrelevant, because the feeling of solidarity is not inherent in pilgrimage, although it may be a by-product. The nature of the social bond between the participants, in other words the feeling of brotherhood and sisterhood, originates in shared religious values, which provide the pilgrim with a cosmological frame of reference and which, in many cases, motivate the pilgrimage in the first place.

Having reviewed the critical remarks on Turner's theory of pilgrimage, I was delighted on his behalf when I found that scholars seem to agree that a pilgrimage is an ellipse. His notion that all pilgrimages are ellipses is psychologically important. His observation that the return road is different from the approach road is correct and significant, because the ellipse metaphor does, in fact, contain binary oppositions such as departure : return, deficiency : deficiency made good, old man/woman : new man/woman, impure : pure, illness : cure, path lost : path found, death : rebirth.

Of all metaphors for life, the most evocative is that of departure, journey and return; (1) the departure, so full of the sadness of separation and excitement about the adventures to come; (2) the journey, a series of hazards and transitions, setbacks and triumphs; (3) the return, marked by final transformation, fulfillment and completion. The longing for adventure seems to underlie all travels, both inner and outer, all ventures into scholarship and literature, music and art, all self-imposed trials and ordeals.

Every pilgrimage begins in a familiar place, in other words at the pilgrim's station in life. Although the motives for going on a pilgrimage vary, as do the moments of departure regarding the pilgrim's stage in life, the underlying motivation for departure nevertheless always seems to be that of perceived deficiency.

Anne Osterrieth distinguished three types of deficiencies that motivated medieval Christian pilgrimages, namely, the sinner seeking salvation, the sick person desiring a bodily cure and the lonely person aspiring towards revelation. In other cultural contexts it may be possible to distinguish other types, such as the cured individual going on a pilgrimage to honour a vow, but they are not relevant here. The point is that the motivation for departure in all cases seems to be some kind of deficiency, and the aim of the pilgrimage is to make good or eliminate that deficiency, a "discovery" confirming its binary character. Hence I concluded: *a pilgrimage forms an ellipse, but is not a transition rite.*

3

I T HAS BEEN CLEARLY STATED THAT the one thing all transition rites have in common is the transition from one social status to another, in other words the crossing of a social threshold. It has been equally clearly stated that this is not the case in pilgrimages. What, then, should we call the quality that distinguishes pilgrimages and which is characteristic only of them?

In answering this question I recalled that Turner, for example, had observed that the pilgrim is confronted by sequences of sacred objects, and that he or she participates in symbolic activities which are believed to be efficacious in changing the inner and, sometimes, the outer condition from sin to grace, or sickness to health. The pilgrim hopes for miracles and transformation of soul or body.

Morinis was also asking the Socratic question. He was searching for the quality that distinguishes pilgrimages from other travels and is characteristic of them. First, after analyzing the material he collected in West Bengal, he complains that, while the journey to the sacred place occurs in all pilgrimages by definition, no qualitative factor is similarly recurrent. Later, to the contrary, he concludes that the common idea underlying all the variety of pilgrimage as a phenomenon is that travelling to a sacred place, where the divine is accessible, can and indeed does bring about a *transformation* in the life of the individual.

Harald Skar confesses in his study of the Andean pilgrimage tradition that, as he took part in the pilgrimage, he experienced a shift from a sedentary situation into a nomadic one, and began to feel inwardly a transformation of spirit and personality. As I read Skar's "confessional" tale I recalled the statement of a Greek student of medicine, who told me that on the Holy Mountain his mind became peaceful. "I found myself as a human being," he said to me in a state of sheer bliss.

From the accounts reviewed above it became clear to me that the one thing in common is the word transformation, which, of course, comes from the Latin word *transformare* and denotes change of character or condition. This is indeed what takes place on a pilgrimage. Anne Osterrieth quite correctly argues that the pilgrim completes the process of spiritual transformation at the pilgrimage site. This last leg of the journey is characterized by both performance and glorification. The quest ends with the establishment of the new identity—spiritual rebirth, as it were. Indeed, a great pilgrimage is an inner struggle, an effort to overcome doubt and any hesitation regarding completing the journey, and it is this trial that transforms the pilgrim.

The quality of pilgrimage, then, is not found in the social process, as Turner argued—paraphrasing the ideas of van Gennep. If we listen attentively to what pilgrims say and what they experience during the pilgrimage, we realize that they experience a *transformation from one level of spirituality to another.* I therefore stated in my encyclopedic entry that spiritual transformation is the specific quality by which pilgrimages do not differ, but are all alike, just as transition from one social status to another was the distinguishing characteristic of transition rites.

Perhaps the best way to illustrate this fact is to recall that there is usually some sort of ritual bathing at the pilgrimage center. In Islam, for example, every pilgrim carries out ablutions before performing the rites of *hadji* at *Ka'bah* in Mecca. Ritual bathing is a very important element in Indian religious behavior, too.

Allow me to demonstrate my point with an example from everyday life in Finland, which, I think, will serve to explain the significance of ritual bathing. A Finn never feels cleaner than after a sauna. The person who comes out of the sauna is a "new" person. The dirtier one was, the cleaner one is now. The contrast counts and marks the difference. The more distinct the contrast, the more miraculous the feeling afterwards. This physical perception seems to explain why some pilgrims experience an ecstatic spiritual transformation at the pilgrimage center, whereas others feel only a moderate spiritual renewal. Those who deem themselves heavy sinners feel much greater relief than those who regard themselves merely as ordinary wrong-doers. The greater the contrast, the more miraculous the experience.

Although there is this difference in the intensity of the perceived spiritual transformation from defilement to purity, from the old person to the new person, the transformative feeling is nevertheless the specific quality of the experience at the pilgrimage center. The feeling of cleanness and purity is not only a mental and spiritual perception, but it is sensed physically too, as after a sauna. Ritual bathing may rightly be apprehended in symbolic terms as a process of death and rebirth. On occasions when an illness has been cured at the pilgrimage center, the pilgrim naturally feels certain that a miracle has happened. Miracles are indeed expected to happen on sacred sites. The agony of toothache is familiar to everyone, as is the miraculous feeling when it is no more. The feeling is paradisiacal. This shift from suffering to bliss seems to be the decisive sign of spiritual transformation.

Understandably therefore, the person who begins a return journey is a "new person" and is symbolically reborn. This rebirth is occasionally also "physical," as when an illness is cured. The return marks the final transformation, spiritual fulfillment and completion of the pilgrimage.

In the last part of the entry I added further paragraphs about pilgrimage in comparative perspectives, as I knew that readers would be interested in learning something about how the journeys differ in various cultures and world religions. It was also justified because, although pilgrimages are universal in form, they are unique in their belief content. From field research among pilgrims in various cultures it is known that pilgrimages vary considerably from one religion to another. A Hindu pilgrimage differs from a Buddhist one, which again is different from

Jewish, Christian or Muslim ones. The pilgrim's perception of deficiency is universal, but beliefs vary about how it can be made good or eliminated.

The religions of the Far East, Hinduism and Buddhism, presuppose a cyclic view of time, in other words a belief in rounds of rebirth (*samsara*) and in release from these rounds. The religions of the Middle East, Judaism, Christianity, and Islam again assume a linear view of time, a belief in a beginning and an end, and in the possibility of transcending that end, in salvation. God is supposed to have created both the world and man as well as woman, and the same God judges whether or not a man or a woman reaches Heaven. This fundamental difference in worldview is, of course, reflected in the way pilgrims conceive of their pilgrimage.

For Hindus, a pilgrimage is meritorious by nature. Visiting sacred places, bathing in holy waters, circumambulating the shrine and the like are generally held automatically to lead to an increase in the individual's merit store. The merit thus accumulated can be applied to bring about changes in the existential conditions of the pilgrim's life in the immediate or distant future, and so in this life or the next.

Although different sub-groups within Hinduism express this process somewhat differently, all nevertheless share the notion that the individual, in the course of many incarnations, is involved in a long spiritual journey in search of the godhead. This journey is the cycle of *samsara*, the wandering of the soul until it becomes spiritually awake in one life. From this perspective, the terrestrial pilgrimage takes its meaning and its effect by bringing the individual *jiva* closer to the deity, effecting a spiritual transformation in the pilgrim. The ultimate goal for a Hindu is to bring the individual soul to oneness with the deity, God.

For a Buddhist, visiting sacred places is also meritorious, because Gautama Buddha is considered to be "spiritually present" in the religious relics and symbols at the pilgrimage centers. The monks who look after the site provide a "field of merit" for the laity. By performing meritorious acts, such as paying homage at sacred centers, giving paraphernalia, meditating and keeping the precepts, the Buddhist pilgrim accumulates merit for his future rebirths and finally for nirvana, or release from the rounds of rebirth, which is a Buddhist's ultimate goal.

For a Jew, a pilgrimage is an offering of sacrifices. By travelling to holy sites, tombs and shrines of *Talmudic* and *Qabbalistic* sages, where they pray, make offerings, and sometimes request divine help in notes left at the site, Jewish pilgrims hope for good luck and remedies for particular misfortunes. The saint is expected to ask God for mercy on behalf of the pilgrim. The ultimate goal in the life of a Jew is to reach Heaven.

For a Christian, a pilgrimage is a form of ascetic practice. It is a penitential act. The fallen man repents his sins and asks for God's forgiveness and mercy. Going on a pilgrimage narrows the gap between the life of Jesus and modern life. Through God's grace the pilgrim, the fallen man, can reach Heaven, which is the ultimate goal in a Christian's life.

For a Muslim, a pilgrimage (*hadji*) is a ritual act of worship. To perform *hadji* is the fifth of the Five Pillars of Islam. It is the duty of every Muslim to make a pilgrimage to Mecca at least once in their adult life. By going on a pilgrimage, the Muslim submits to God's will, which is the very essence of Islam. The ultimate goal of a Muslim is reach Heaven.

I concluded the entire entry as follows.

> A pilgrimage is the outer manifestation of an inner journey, often referred to as an allegory of the soul's journey to God. Thus it is cosmologically meaningful in the perspectives of salvation and enlightenment. The height of the journey is the arrival at the pilgrimage site and the encounter with the divine. There the pilgrim perceives the gap between what he should be (according to the religious tradition) and what he really is; that is, he suddenly realizes the discrepancy between precept and practice. This experience is the very essence of a pilgrimage, because what has been experienced cannot become unexperienced, what

has been seen cannot become unseen, what has been realized cannot become unrealized. The old person is dead, a new person is born. The world is seen through newly opened eyes. The pilgrim feels a persistent longing for "original" religiosity. The mundane values of the previous life style are abandoned and replaced by values that enhance spiritual development. The pilgrimage is complete.

Summary

1. The quality of a pilgrimage is the pilgrim's experience of spiritual transformation; that is, a shift from worldliness towards spirituality;

2. A pilgrimage should be conceived and defined as a spiritual transformation journey;

3. Although a pilgrim is usually in company, sometimes with thousands of other pilgrims, each pilgrim nevertheless considers the endeavor to be a private undertaking; the choice to go on a pilgrimage is individual, spontaneous and voluntary; a travel incognito;

4. A pilgrimage route forms an ellipse with the sequence structure departure-journey-return;

5. The ellipse metaphor of pilgrimage epitomizes the binary character of the pilgrimage route, i.e. departure : return, deficiency : deficiency made good, old person : new person, death : rebirth, and so forth;

6. The journey—the transformative phase between departure and return—provides a period of reflection, during which the pilgrim mirrors and reviews his life, perceives the discrepancy between precept and practice, and begins to long to bridge the gap; and

7. Regardless of whether the pilgrim experiences an ecstatic or a moderate spiritual transformation when encountering the divine, the result nevertheless usually leads to some change of attitude and lifestyle.

While I was reading the final proofs of my entry, a slight dissatisfaction crept into my mind. There was nothing wrong with my text. It filled the expectations of what an encyclopedic entry should be like. It represented the so-called conventional wisdom of our time. In these respects everything was in order.

Nevertheless, the dry matter-of-factness and impersonality bothered me. My text was detached and objective. It reflected book-learning. Any specialist in the field could have written it. There is no storyteller in an encyclopedia. All entries are statements of fact written more or less from "no one's point of view." As literary genres the entries are not suitable for communicating the kind of knowledge about pilgrimage as a human endeavor that I realized I missed when I was reading the proofs once more. It ignored the field experiences that lay behind my understanding of what pilgrimage is all about. I could sense neither the presence of the author nor the pulse of pilgrimage. A reader familiar with my style of writing might perhaps occasionally recognize the writer, but on the whole, the entry was merely bookish, a literary product belonging solely to the academic world. To sense the experiences and the presence of a pilgrim or pilgrimage as a human endeavour was next to impossible. This made me dissatisfied.

What truly disturbed me was the enormous gap I sensed between the academic explanation and the empirical perception. Anyone who wants to learn about pilgrimage is, of course, well advised to go on one to a holy site and thereby find out for himself or herself what it is really all about. To someone who is completely ignorant of pilgrimage as a phenomenon, the entry certainly provides some basic information and a good starting point for further reading. In this respect, any entry of this kind is justified and useful.

However, the fact remains that knowledge can be communicated in the form of an entry, while experience cannot. Everyone has to find out through personal experience. There is no other way. The only way to understand life is through living it so that in the course of time experiences teach us how to cope with day-to-day nuisances and troubles, sometimes with a little help from our friends. My discontentment with the entry was, for the most part, due to the fact that I read it from the perspective of someone who had a thorough personal perception of pilgrimage. No wonder it was dull. The richness of my experiences and the wisdom of spiritual life mirrored in the words of the Athonites could not be embedded in the kind of literary genre an entry is supposed to be. This discrepancy irritated me.

Jacob Bronowski (d. 1974) wrote at length about creativity in both Science and the Arts. He defines art as a product in which we can sense the presence of a single mind. This means that the author or creator is present in the art so that it is immediately felt to be his or her work, and that this presence testifies to its authenticity. He also claimed that it was, as a matter of fact, impossible to copy an artist's work and remain undetected in the long run. The specialist will always be able to detect the fraud. This also holds true in literature and poetry. The presence of a single mind is like a fingerprint or DNA sample that reveals the creator.

The presence of the author is more easily felt in literature and poetry than in an encyclopedic entry, because in the latter the form and style are restricted and standardized. This now troubled me. It was not that I would have liked to experience a smug sense of self-satisfaction in leaving my own fingerprints on the text itself and not only in the list of references. The problem was much deeper: how was I to communicate to the readers my insight into pilgrimage as a perceivable religious phenomenon?

In his book *Studies in Words*, Clive Staples Lewis (d. 1963) argues that we understand words much better when we have met them alive, in their native habitat as it were. The information and knowledge we get from dictionaries and encyclopedias is, of course, general and useful, but the precise meaning is revealed only when the phenomenon of pilgrimage touches us personally on a journey to a sacred site. We cannot gain a sense of going on a pilgrimage merely by reading: experience in the field is required, and in fact is the *sine quo non* of understanding pilgrimage as a religious phenomenon.

As I was pondering these questions I recalled an article I wrote some years ago about my own experiences of pilgrimage on the Holy Mountain during Easter 1993. This article was at that time regarded by some colleagues as daring. A few even considered me lost as a "scientist," a word much used in Finland instead of the traditional and apt concept of "scholar," which I still prefer. In humanities we are scholars, in natural science scientists. This distinction is important, because it concerns not the method, but the kind of knowledge we wish to obtain. Anyone could sense the presence of the author in that article. It was of the kind no one else could have written, and I doubt could even copy in the future. I felt a sweet sense of satisfaction as I recalled it.

Pilgrimage Experienced

I

THE "NO ONE'S POINT OF VIEW" IN MY encyclopedic entry troubled me so much that on the evening before I left for Ouranoupolis I reread my "confessional" tale *Becoming the pilgrim to be interviewed*. I read it through, completely absorbed. I noticed how the persistent feeling of discontent gradually loosened its grip on me. Inspired by what I had perceived on the Holy Mountain, I had deliberately searched for a new way to express my thoughts. I oscillated in the article between being an anthropologist of religion and a pilgrim experiencing pilgrimage en route, because when doing field work or rather being-in-the-field one cannot avoid fluctuating between these two roles.

These, then, were the circumstances of my pilgrimage. I had just finished proofreading my first volume on Athonite monasticism, and the second, dealing exclusively with pilgrimage, was in typescript. Tired, I finally managed to leave my duties and revisit the Holy Mountain for what was supposed to be a routine check of some of my field notes. I had every reason to expect this to be like any of my other previous sojourns, which had been annual early-September two-week retreats since 1984. This one, though, was to be at Easter, as indeed had been the case in 1988. There was nothing to suggest that anything extraordinary would happen.

While proofreading the chapter on monasticism and mythology, I once more read the Athonite interpretation of the Fall, the *Unseen Warfare*—the spiritual struggle every monk has to endure to attain deification, *theosis*—and the Psalms of the Divine Liturgy described and analyzed in my study.

In his role theory, Hjalmar Sundén considers this kind of re-reading to be the *conditio sine qua non* for experiencing a personal living God. Although familiar with his lines of thought, I did not deliberately think about them then; the re-reading merely happened to provide an appropriate preparation. Sundén convincingly points out that a religious experience does not consist of specific feelings. It is rather a matter of *perception*, the process whereby sensory stimulation is translated into organized or meaningful experience, in other words the intuitive recognition of a "truth." This he demonstrates with the concept of role. Taking a role, he argues, inevitably involves anticipating a partner, an "other," in relation to whom the role is played. When, for example, a child pretends to be a seller, he or she anticipates a customer, and when changing to the role of a customer, he or she anticipates a seller. This duality, Sundén argues, is an inherent part of any role. It contains specific expectations as to what the "other" should or will do. Role-taking, he concludes, implies not only a readiness to act, but also a standing-by position for perception.

The biblical tradition provides us with behavioral models and role models of pious men and women who have entered into dialogue with God and experienced His presence, roles ready to be identified with and re-enacted. The *Psalms* have proven to be a particularly good springboard for role re-enacting, an expression I use in preference to Sundén's role-taking. My own field research illustrates that it is a matter not of intentionally adopting or taking a role, but of suddenly finding oneself re-enacting one by means of words conceived of within a specific interactional system, as it were, the human role in relation to the divine Partner, God.

The decisive condition required for the role re-enacting to take place is the being-in-need-of situation, in other words a distressful predicament involving an unyielding longing and need for a solution—a release of tension! Verbalizing his experiences, Isaac Singer wrote: "Whenever things grow extremely bad and I think that the end is near, something inevitable happens that seems a miracle."

In a situation of utmost need, not seldom at the edge of despair, what comes to the mind of a religious-person-to-be who has patiently been brought up or dwelled in a religious frame of reference and internalized a religious discourse are the promises God has fulfilled to biblical persons, in other words roles. Rather than giving up all hope or relying merely on their own shaky abilities, they humbly surrender to what, in the light of the religious tradition, has proven to be reliable and trustworthy. The line of thought seems to be that as God saved then, God will also do so now, if only we trust and rely on Him. No matter how hopeless the situation may seem, we expect that the promises will eventually be fulfilled.

These are the role aspects that, according to Sundén, provide *un système aperceptif* for the soul to be touched and moved by a personal living God. This happens especially through hearing words because, as Martin Luther correctly pointed out, it is through the ear (*per auditum*) that Christ enters the soul of man. Therefore, by reading the text aloud and by listening attentively to its words, one eventually finds oneself in the presence of God, *coram Deo*. "God is omnipresent," Luther states, and he continues, "but when he is present to you (personally) it is entirely a different matter." By that *coram Deo* experience one becomes totally and unreservedly convinced of the existence of a personal living God, an experience that completely restructures one's way of conceiving of the world and one's own position in it. Suddenly everything looks different and there is a profound purpose in life and in nature, as witnessed by St. Augustine in the *Confessions* (1:1–2). It is as if the pieces of the puzzle were suddenly falling into place and the universe of religious beliefs and symbols were becoming existentially meaningful.

2

NOT MANY THEORIES IN comparative religion have stood the test of time. Aside from Arnold van Gennep's theory on rites of passage, Hjalmar Sundén's so-called role theory has proven to be an indispensable analytical model for understanding religious experiences. The word "experience" here is a keyword. Sundén wrote his first and most lucid essay on this in Swedish. He used the word *erfarenhet*, and the word *Erfahrung* in German, rather than *upplevelse* or the respective German term *Erlebnis*, which have almost the same meaning. This is somewhat problematic in English, because there is only one word for experience and not two as in Swedish and German.

Erfahrung does not refer to a state of mind or a feeling forming part of the inner religious life, but rather implies actual observation of or practical acquaintance with facts or events. It denotes a cognitive *perception*, as in expressions such as "I know from my own bitter experience," "practical experience tells me," and "I have gained by that experience."

This, then, is how I jotted down my perceptions in my diary after my pilgrimage on the Holy Mountain during Easter 1993:

"As soon as I boarded the Athos ferry with more than one hundred other pilgrims, my mood changed. With one book on Mount Athos in print and the other practically finished, I was no longer driven by demands to collect data or to accomplish a specific program of field research. On the contrary, I was feeling great relief simply in being one of them, though a foreigner among pious Greek pilgrims. This freedom from stress took me by surprise. It gave me exceptional pleasure and satisfaction. Although a doubt or two crept into my mind whether I would have the strength to walk the heavy paths on the mountain between the monasteries, I soon concluded that there was no turning back, not that I had any second thoughts about it, and now I am glad I did not. I no longer needed to be the participant-observer-programmed anthropologist, but merely an ordinary human being... on a pilgrimage with a personal quest, a personal spiritual journey.

"During the seven days I was allowed to tour the monasteries on the Holy Mountain, I underwent the severe hardship of an austere pilgrimage: walking, fasting, attending prolonged services, getting cold, falling ill, and, eventually, experiencing the blessing of recovery and salvation. What was to be smooth field work turned out to be a genuine pilgrim's ordeal.

"I visited five monasteries on foot in four days. When I arrived at Iviron after hours of lonely walking on the narrow winding mountain paths since the early morning, first in the boiling sun and then in icy rain—because the Easter weather is so unpredictable in northern Greece—I was already quite exhausted from the excessive sweating. I had not eaten a hot meal during my tour, only cold bean soup, bread and some wine. The guest master monk, Father Nikon, immediately showed me to the church with no further ado to celebrate vespers. I stood wet and cold for about three hours, until I was shivering and feeling so stiff that, in order to survive, I went out of the church and walked around it, at first slowly, then faster about half a dozen times to warm myself up. Then back again into the church I went.

"I felt that the holy relics of the spiritual fathers of the past also obliged me to try my best. It is not the dead bones or the skull that is venerated in the relics, but the powerful energy of the Holy Spirit in them. This I knew from my previous studies and therefore I had taken part in all the services and in three all-night vigils, agrypnía. To my own surprise I felt a need in my heart to open myself to God by making the sign of the cross and kissing the icons, as do the monks and pious pilgrims. This happened of its own accord and I simply went along with it.

"After vespers, Father Nikon showed me to the room where I was to lodge. It had four beds, the others being occupied by middle-aged Greeks. One of them snored loudly like a hippopotamus, another went time and again to the toilet or walked restlessly about. The third tried persistently to make conversation with me: 'Mr. Finland, what do you think, is there only one God or are there many gods? Is the God of the Hindus the same God as our God?' As all of us were taking part in the all-night vigils more or less 'idiorhythmically,' the door creaked all through the night; it was impossible to sleep.

"Good Friday, my fifth day on the Holy Mountain. After a prolonged liturgy, all of us pilgrims were given bread, halvah, olives and water, which we ate standing up. I was already weak. Freezing cold as it was in the refectory, and hungry as we all were, we frantically stuffed our mouths, our hands shaking, with as much bread and halvah as we possibly could, not knowing when we were to be given our next meal, or when the reader, Father Arsenios, who was reading from the lives of the saints while we were eating, would stop his recital as a sign for us to finish eating.

"During the day, all of us rested in our beds. Like the Greeks, I, too, changed into my pyjamas, and there we were, all of us, lying between the sheets. One was reading the Divine Liturgy, another was deep in sleep, the third once more tried to have a conversation with me: 'Mr. Finland, what do you think, is there life after death? Mr. Finland, what do you think…' I was too tired to answer his questions, of which there seemed to be no end. 'I don't know,' was my laconic reply as I pretended to fall asleep.

"It occurred to me that it was like being in a hospital; the white walls, the simple beds, the sandals beneath each bed and the expectant atmosphere—everything reminded me of that. It was as if we were waiting for major surgery, which in a way we were—the resurrection of Christ.

"This was how, in 1993, we prepared ourselves for Easter service. At one point my temperature was rising. Luckily, because I knew Father Nikon, I managed to get hot tea, an aspirin and some *raki* to warm myself up. I felt somewhat better later in the evening and dragged myself to the service, which some hours earlier I was afraid would be impossible. Although I do not conceive of myself as a particularly sinful person, perhaps no more than any ordinary man, I was touched and moved by the angelic *antiphonic* singing of the choirs, and especially by the words

'*Kyrie, eleison*' ('Lord, have mercy on me'), repeated perpetually until I felt absorbed in them. They became 'my own words.' The singing was so beautiful and soothing that tears kept coming to my eyes.... I so badly needed the strength to survive this journey, and even more I longed for relief from the anguished nagging distress and the tension of a personal problem I had been living with in recent years. While my heart cried '*Kyrie, eleison,*' my soul sensed the profound meaning of these words, which became flesh in me, made their home in me, as Sundén quite aptly argued and understood. Then it did not matter at all whether I had the strength to survive the service or not, as long as I could feel and be convinced of the presence and mercy of God.

"The resurrection of Christ was celebrated outside the church. Each of us carried a candle and sang 'Christ is risen!' ('*Christòs anésti.*'). When, in the early morning hours, I finally went to bed, all I heard was '*Kyrie, eleison.*' I could not sleep because I began to worry how I would be able to walk with my heavy rucksack the next day in my feverish state. It was ten kilometers, about five hours, across the mountain to the harbour of Daphne where the ferry would take me to the mainland.

"Next morning, Father Nikon gave me some tea, an aspirin and two eggs saying, 'Be blessed.' These words had a special meaning for me then: it was as if God himself had answered my cries for mercy, and it was also as if thereby he wanted to comfort me and dismiss my doubts about my return. I knew there was no way I could walk the whole distance uphill—I was too exhausted. Before I left the monastery, Father Nikon reminded me again: 'Every step on the Holy Maintain is protected by the Blessed Virgin.'

"When I reached the road, a pick-up truck came as if from nowhere. The driver offered me a seat in the back beside an Athenian with a bad back and a Cretan with a fractured wrist. During our one-hour ride through the mountain, in the back of the pick-up, under the open sky, gazing in wonder at the sun's rays peeping down from between dark rainy clouds—an altar-fresco indeed—I felt blessed in my heart: I knew I was going to recover and be saved from this trial. I was so moved that in my mind I spontaneously uttered several times: 'Father, you granted me mercy' [My line of the dialogue according to Sundén].

"When the ferry eventually landed in Ouranoupolis and I took my first steps on the jetty, the village looked different, strange and unreal. My worlds were turned around. The Athonite world had become my world and, for a moment, the mundane world seemed the strange place I was to visit. I had perceived a personal relation to God, something I had never done before, and that moved me thoroughly and convinced me of the existence of a personal living God. Perhaps my experience was not as dramatic as the cases described and analyzed by Sundén, but it was turbulent enough to convince me of the validity of his theory. I had indeed inadvertently found myself in a biblical role, so to speak. My first thought was that I needed to get my encounter on paper as soon as possible. And this I did."

3

I STILL FOUND THE FIELD-NOTE-BASED account of my *Becoming the pilgrim to be interviewed* moving after all these years. I had not forgotten my experience, but somehow in the midst of all my daily duties, my various obligations had occupied my mind to the extent that I had not thought much about it for some years. It is also likely that the Easter pilgrimage was a resolution of a kind, and there was nothing left to trouble me any more. Be that as it may.

Twenty years ago, when I first interviewed pilgrims to Athos about their experiences, the aforementioned Greek student of medicine said to me: "It is impossible for me to translate my thoughts into words. It was the kind of experience you can live, not explain—I found myself there, I returned to my roots as a human being." Now, after my own experience, I no longer needed to ask questions. I had first-hand knowledge. I had myself become the pilgrim to be interviewed.

The far-reaching implications of my encounter with the pilgrims to Athos are not easily understandable to natural scientists. This also applies to *positivists* and *cognitivists*, who look at the world from the viewpoint of the methodic processes of natural science. They do not see the crucial importance of distinguishing between methodic, hermeneutic and existential truths.

Methodic truth is exactitude arrived at by methods analogous to those used in natural science. *Hermeneutic truth*, on the other hand, refers to the precise understanding of a word, for example, and that is not the same as explaining. Understanding is not the result of a linear cognitive process, whereby we proceed from one clear idea to the next new and even more lucid one, but it is rather "hitting the nail on the head" regarding understanding the authentic sense of the word expressed. It is an insight, a linguistic enlightenment if you like, and this is crucial to understanding pilgrimage as a human phenomenon.

Scholars with the methodical horizon of a scientist or positivist have difficulties in "understanding" what anthropological field work is all about. Examining chromosomes and studying the culture of our fellow humans are two entirely different scholarly enterprises, not least due to the difference in subject matter. For the former we need a microscope through which we can observe and register the chromosomes, the thread-like structures found in all living cells that carry hereditary information in the form of genes. We sit comfortably behind our optical research instrument and the chromosomes are on plates in front of our lens. The observations are objective and scientific. They can be checked by scholars who repeat the same methodical procedure because the structure, or chemical patterns, and location of the chromosomes are predictable.

To study the culture of fellow humans, on the other hand, requires more than standing aloof on a mountain slope and registering through a pair of binoculars the hordes of pilgrims heading for the Holy Mountain of Athos, for instance. Counting the number of pilgrims on the road, recording their dress and equipment, age, fitness and style of walking, deducing their nationality on the basis of observation, and so forth, would be quite feasible from afar, but irrelevant if we wish to know *what it means* to go on a pilgrimage. The meaning is to be found in the universe of the words used by the pilgrims, and to hit the nail on the head in terms of understanding the word is to perceive it in its (etymological) tradition and in dialogue with its present-day context.

We need not view pilgrims from a distance for the simple reason that we are able to get closer to the object or rather the subject of our study. This makes a decisive difference in the dialectic between subject matter and method. We cannot become a chromosome among chromosomes and take part in their activities, but we can and should join the group of pilgrims and become a pilgrim among pilgrims in search of the *authentic word* to elucidate the *sense* of going on a pilgrimage.

The study of fellow pilgrims, then, differs from chromosome studies in that the distinctive character of our work is not restricted to registering and testing—a binocular approach, so to speak. It cannot be reduced to abstraction and proposition by conceptualizing historical life. It allows, and in fact requires, participant observation, including free and guided interviews, self-observation, self-analysis and reflection, during the actual, tangible day-to-day reality of a pilgrimage, which is the anthropological method of field research. Each scholar is his or her own empirical research instrument. This distinctiveness of fieldwork has epistemological and method(olog)ical consequences.

Field research is a truly human endeavour. It is not only a case of counting numbers, scrutinizing structures and analyzing functions, in other words recording statistics and quantitative averages, but also involves concentrating on people's linguistic sense or understanding—in this case of the humane quality or meaningfulness of going on a pilgrimage. We can and indeed should ask what it is like to be a pilgrim. For this we need to abandon the pre-programmed and detached standpoint of our inherited (methodical) horizon—to break out of our "I-centerdness," as it were—to become involved with and to surrender to the religious frame of reference, and to accept the possibility that what the God pilgrims speak about really might exist in their *existential reality*. To study fellow humans, in my case pilgrims to Athos, therefore, implies living as close to them as possible and thereby becoming familiar, also on a personal level, with their religious language and mentality—the pilgrims' habit, as it were—and with the religious universe on which their pilgrimage is based. A detached approach to this kind of research will not do. We need to become thoroughly involved with the religious language of the subject in question.

One fundamental difference between examining chromosomes and studying pilgrimage, then, is in the testing. Whereas in the former it is possible to be detached, in the latter, where the aim is to understand fellow humans, testing the "truth," or rather "increasing our understanding" of our humanness, requires *temporal* involvement, surrendering to the linguistic belief system concerned and making that universe our own (for the time of the study) so that the event of understanding can take place. This implies unreserved participation, suspension of disbelief or controlled subjectivity, and discernment.

To look at pilgrims only from afar would be negligent, given that there are opportunities to live the daily life of pilgrims by walking miles in their shoes, perceiving what they experience, discussing their ordeals, and learning about this specific form of human culture by personally undergoing the trials and rewards of pilgrimage. In other words, it is a question of being there en route, which is the *sine qua non* of sensing the spiritual reward of a pilgrimage and hence of understanding it as a human phenomenon.

The distinction between the field researcher speaking as a scholar and the field researcher speaking as a pilgrim is fundamental in analyzing the field-research process of becoming the pilgrim to be interviewed. There is an analogical distinction between Dante as a pilgrim and Dante as an author. I would therefore like to suggest the concept "living the part" to designate the process whereby the field researcher inadvertently finds that he or she has temporarily adopted the "internal frame of reference" of, in my case, the Athos pilgrim, without losing his or her own identity. There are two phases of participant observation in this process: preparation, involving living the linguistic part, and perceptive culmination, an unexpected peak of experience, during which the distinction between self and other is temporarily dissolved and, to one's own surprise, one becomes "the part, the pilgrim to be studied." One feels touched and moved by the atmosphere in which God is believed to be present, irrespective of whether, in general terms, God exists or not. This process is more or less unexpected and inevitable, especially when the scholar is unprogrammed and ready to allow for the emergence of the pilgrim within. The by-product of my surprising experience was an insightful empirical understanding of the Greek word for pilgrim, *proskynitís*, a knowledge different and more substantial than that obtained from the lexicon. Indeed, it is relevant to distinguish between the lexical and the empirical meanings of the word *proskynitís*.

Thus, my comparative approach to the scholar-pilgrim presupposed looking at pilgrims to Athos first from the perspective of the Greek *proskynitís*, then from the perspective of the Roman Catholic *peregrinus*, and finally from a withdrawn point of detachment. In this way I could compare and scrutinize the similarities and differences in viewpoints and in the connotations of the words with reference to my own field experiences. This is how, as a by-product of participant observation, one reaches a personally witnessed or first-hand experiential and yet scientific understanding of what I will call here the insightful or empirical meaning of the word *proskynitís*, in other words, the religious experience and phenomenon Greek pilgrims refer to with the word *proskynitís*.

Sundén's role theory proved to be indispensable in interpreting my "becoming the pilgrim to be interviewed" or, to paraphrase Nils G. Holm, my finding myself enacting the "inner existence space" of a Greek pilgrim. By perceiving the empirical meaning of what the word stands for under my own skin in terms of Sundén's theoretical discussion, I sensed and, so I like to believe, understood the universe of the spirituality embraced in the word *proskynitís*. Kissing the icons, venerating the relics, kneeling down before the abbot (*hegoumenos*) and praying for the Lord's mercy (*Kyrie, eleison*) are only the outward manifestations of a profoundly humble attitude before a sacred universe and before "our Lord." These acts mirror the opening up of our hearts in front of the God the Athonites are talking about, and before praying for mercy and grace to enter one's soul, the aim of which is communion with God and deification, *theosis*. It is the perception of transformation from one level of spirituality to another, to a more profound and lasting spirituality, that attracts the Athonite pilgrims, Greeks and foreigners alike, to annual or recurrent journeys to the Holy Mountain of Athos. Today more than 400,000 men a year visit the site. This should be enough to prove that it is of general interest to understand the phenomenon. What is it in pilgrimage that makes it meaningful, even compelling?

My becoming the pilgrim to be interviewed demonstrates how field research involves being in the midst of a psychodynamic triangle, the extreme points of which could be called involvement, detachment and commitment.

Involvement is a precondition for all research. You have to get involved in your subject and its inherent problems, with all the emotional and ethical tensions that meddling in affairs involves. Walking on the Holy Mountain with other pilgrims, I shared their experiences. It was true involvement to be exhausted by walking the paths between the monasteries, to be welcomed by the guest master, to be shown to a room together with the other pilgrims, to wash after hours of sweating under the scorching Aegean sun, to rest awhile, to take part in all the services in the church, to eat communal meals with the monks, to listen to the pilgrims' experiences, to sleep in the same room with them, and to follow the pilgrims' routines both en route and at the sacred center. But most of all, the words spoken by the pilgrims begin to mean more in the field context than they do in the lexicon.

Detachment is the *sine qua non* of all critical research. It involves the human capacity for (temporary) freedom from emotional aspects and feelings of affinity. It implies looking at things from a distance with discernment and sound judgement, in other words understanding. This is done in the anthropological study of religion by keeping a diary, collecting verbatim statements, writing down observations and reflections, and reading books on the subject. Keeping a diary has become somewhat an obsession of mine, a way of clearing my thoughts, of coping with emotions and perceptions by dressing them in words, a means of becoming familiar with foreign habits and slowly making myself cozy in a strange milieu. Above all, I know of nothing more pleasant than reading my notes when I have returned home and, in the midst of the daily grind deciding to make a nostalgic trip back to the field by re-living my experiences during the previous summer. In the field, it is the diarist "I" who is at work, the writer or scholar "I" taking over only afterwards, sitting at a desk, absorbed in *otium litteratum.*

Commitment denotes the subjectivity that is the result of emotional involvement. If you are committed, you will have a vested interest in the issue whether you admit it or not, and that is a serious hindrance to critical and balanced research.

Therefore, the first thing you need to do is to get involved in your subject, and then to commit yourself only to sincere, simple and sensitive seeking for the hermeneutical truth—in this case in the words expressed by the pilgrims. From time to time you will need to detach yourself from your involvement and tendency toward commitment to get a more distant view of what you have studied. This means that you must hover between involvement and detachment, constantly taking care not to fall into the trap of commitment. What you really need is sound and clear discernment in recording and scrutinizing the process in question.

To avoid any misunderstandings, I must stress that the issue here is not and never can be whether, in general terms or ultimately, God exists or not. It is only the fact that, *under given conditions,* we perceive the presence of a personal living God within the Judeo-Christian-Islamic worldview, or religious frame of reference as Sundén prefers to call it. This I know, not only from interviewing other pilgrims who dress their experiences in words and religious terms, but also from personal experience.

The point, then, is that, apart from a so-called scientific truth, there is what I would prefer to call a hermeneutical truth and an existential or subjective truth. Hermeneutical truth is not the same as subjective truth. In order not to dwell on misleading trivial lines of thought, it may be conceived of as a truth that, under given conditions—in this case within the framework of the Orthodox belief system—is perceivable and even vital for human existence.

To understand other people's existential truth by means of philosophical hermeneutics will prove to be vital. Many wars have been fought over it, and millions of people have been killed because they were considered infidels. What is more worrying is that even today, millions of people are prepared to die—and what is worse, to kill—for their beliefs. It explains the dynam-ics behind the terrible and terrorizing deeds carried out in the name of God, including genocide and religious wars, and also the living examples of the good Samaritan such as St. Francis and Mother Teresa. This shows how powerful the existential truth is—recall Luther's statement, "…but when God is present to you it is entirely a different matter"—and therefore getting an insight into the dynamics within the human soul may one day prove to be of crucial importance for the survival of mankind.

God surely exists for the person who so believes, and this fact is as elementary as any scientific truth can ever be. For the devout it is a personally experienced empirical truth, fundamen-tal to that person's existence. It gives life its meaning and direc-tion, in other words its generative drive and goal.

By inadvertently becoming the pilgrim to be interviewed, I learned that surrendering meant having a dialogue within a specific discourse. Discourse, from the Latin *discursus*, literally means running to and fro, hence conversation (around a topic); this implies *all* of the connected expressions, statements and con-cepts. One example is moral, scientific or religious discourse. In a narrow sense, we may speak about a Christian, Muslim or Bud-dhist discourse, and even more specifically of a Greek Orthodox, Shia or Theravada discourse. The basic line of thought here is that our relation to reality is *always* expressed through discourse, and that the discourse concerned *dictates our sense of reality* to the extent that we are ensnared by it. A lack of understanding, or misunderstanding, is accordingly the result when, in our com-munication with other people, we are in different discourses or, to put it in everyday terms, when we are not on the same wave-length because of different frames of reference. The aim of dia-logue in field work is therefore to bridge that gap and prepare the way for understanding.

4

ARISTOTLE BEGINS HIS *Metaphysics* by stating that "seeing" has priority over all other senses because "sight best helps us to know things, and reveals many distinctions." In his discussion of "hearing," he says that he who hears, hears thereby somewhat *more*. In other words, he also hears what cannot be seen, namely, everything that can be thought of by means of language. This implies that we see not only the visible world but also the universe we try to understand through hearing language.

Hearing embraces the whole universe of the language of our predecessors, and the means by which they have understood the human condition in this world. It is worthwhile reminding ourselves that we also find the distinction between the visible and the invisible world in the Christian Creed: "I believe in one God, Father Almighty, Maker of Heaven and Earth and of all things visible and invisible." When we talk about "hearing the word," we talk about *disclosing things invisible*.

The human voice gives names to things by means of words. The meaning of the Greek word for name, *ónoma*, is not equivalent to the word "name" in terms of the name by which we are called, our family name or given first name. *Ónoma* means *more* than that. It denotes every noun in the sense that it is a call. Every word as a noun calls us in the same way as someone calls us by our name. This means that when we use a word, we call someone or something. Apart from that, we also say something more, namely what we mean by what we say, in other words the message of our call. The voice tells us something, but it is not the same as the voice of a bird's enticement or warning. The human voice tells us more in that it says something by means of words that disclose what is meant. Allow me to give you an example.

René is an ordinary French name; spelled with one "é" it is a boy's name, but when spelled *Renée*, it is a girl's name. Before I was baptized, I was only a boy. After my baptism, I was no longer merely a boy, but a particular boy called *René*. When people wanted to talk to me, they thereafter called René. In other words they called my name, the name by which I was to be called and by which I was expected to respond—to answer. If, in the same room, there were another boy or girl with the same name, the caller would have to add my family name to avoid misunderstanding. This also applies when I send a postcard to someone. I cannot take it for granted that I am the only *René* the receiver knows. Therefore, I have to add my family name.

René is not, however, merely someone's name. It is also a noun with an etymology or history, originating in the Latin word *renatus* with the meanings "born again," "rise again" and "grow again." Thus the word *René* at once embodies another dimension of meaning, not only the name of a certain boy or man, but also refers to the qualities of becoming something again.

At this point, a brief illustrative excursus will clarify my point. In Finland, as elsewhere, people often misspell my name as *Renè*, *Rène*, *Réne*, and so forth. For many years I have been teaching my students how to spell my name correctly, and also about its etymology. This is necessary. If they cannot spell my name correctly, it reveals that they do not understand the word *René*. The right spelling does not, of course, automatically mean that the speller understands the word in the sense of becoming aware of its meaning(s) in the spelling of it. Nevertheless, the correct spelling is certainly the *sine qua non* for understanding the word. This has something to do with the fact that, as humans, we may be alert to a message, or we may be in a listless state or simply uninterested, and therefore unable to hear what is said.

Moreover, for the sake of argument, let us suppose that my parents gave me the name *René* not only because it sounded nice or because it was the name of some ancestor in our family, but because it was the name of a saint and my birth was a miracle. Perhaps the birth was difficult. Perhaps my parents desperately wanted to have a boy. Be that as it may, my birth and survival seemed to them a miracle, a true "rebirth," and therefore an existential necessity dictated that my name was to be *René* within the horizon of the Roman Catholic conception of Christianity. If this had been the case, which would not have been unheard of, to say *René* would have meant much more to my parents than it means to someone who does not use the name as a religious symbol referring to a specific experience.

René thus has many meanings. This is the case with every word used as a noun. This state of affairs decisively affects our interpretation and understanding of the word. Someone familiar with the Theosophical tradition and the doctrine of rebirth may conceive of the word *René* from within the Theosophical horizon, and therefore entirely miss the point of the word's *authentic* meaning regarding the thing at stake. It is therefore essential to be familiar with the word and its history, as well as with its dimensions of meaning, its worldview horizon as it were, in order to understand what someone means in using the word *René*, for example.

Furthermore, we have to realize that words are symbols in the same hypothetical sense as if my parents had experienced my birth as a miracle. There are numerous cases exemplifying this point in the history of religions. Haralds Biezais (d. 1995) speaks of "existential necessities" when referring to the birth of symbols: the cross is a religious symbol carved out of existential necessity because Christ died on a cross; the wheel is a Buddhist symbol because Gautama Buddha is said to have set in motion the Wheel of Truth. By the same token, *René* is a name given out of existential necessity in a case in which the parents conceived of the birth as a miracle. It does not matter if, in medical terms and within the horizon of natural sciences, the birth was a miracle or not. What matters is the existential truth my parents experienced, in other words, their belief that it was a miracle, the result of which was the fact that I was baptized and given the name *René*.

Thus the word in its nominative sense communicates not merely a call, but much more. It always embodies a universe of conceptions and symbols, a worldview, communicated to us by the one using the word. This is also the case when we use words in everyday life. Someone may use my name *René*, and misspell it, while someone else who knows how it should be spelled immediately realizes that the name is being used carelessly without a thorough understanding of the word. The one familiar with the word *René* therefore hears more than the one who is not. Equally, the one familiar with the name and with the life histories of the saints will hear even more.

The Invitation

I

IN OURANOUPOLIS, TOO, I KEEP to my routine of going for half-an-hour's brisk walk first thing in the morning to get enough oxygen into my lungs for the working hours before noon. Now the morning shift involves merely jotting down thoughts in my diary. What can you do about your habits? We are not only spiritual but also aging beings. This fact has been brought home to me in recent years as close friends have died, reminding me of my own mortality.

I no longer find it so easy to go on foot along the long winding and often relentless paths on the edges of the mountain cliffs. This is a good reason for taking exercise in Ouranoupolis by walking from the village to the border and back in order to get used to the heat and the sun. It is about two miles to the border. The sandy road passes through fields of olive trees and vineyards. The dark purple grapes are already ripe, hanging temptingly in bunches in the sunlight, reminding me of the Fall: "The fruit would be good to eat; it was pleasing to the eye and desirable for the knowledge it could give." As these thoughts entered my mind I began to walk more briskly, as I find it hard to resist temptation. I must confess that I have sometimes found the grapes irresistible on my way back, especially when there has been no wind, and the sun has been almost unbearably hot and my mouth completely dry due to the dust from the road. Then, crossing myself first, I have taken a few grapes as "blessings" given to me by God. The juice feels paradisiacal and many a thankful thought is directed to the farmer, who has unknowingly become the good Samaritan.

The wind from the Aegean Sea rarely finds its way to the road that follows the valley between the small hills. The air is usually dry and hot as it is reflected from the sandy road. Whenever a lorry passes by I find myself walking in the midst of a cloud of dust. No wonder the mouth dries up. Apart from these incidents, I am totally surrounded by the voices of nature: it is so quiet, and not even the dogs watching over the vineyards bark at me as we have long since become friends. On my first day there was a wild dog barking rather aggressively as I passed his patch, but I commanded him in Greek, in an equally angry tone, to sit down and to my surprise that is what he did. Since then we have become friends and the dog usually accompanies me to the border and back. We exchange a few barking words now and again, but on the whole the walk is as pleasant as it can get.

Years ago I discovered that walking is much more rewarding than jogging. Jogging is, of course, appropriate if you want to improve your fitness, but if your aim is to reflect on the apt expression of your thoughts and to find the most suitable wording for your ideas, walking promotes just that. This is not my discovery. Aristotle (d. 322 BC) realized long ago that walking stimulates thinking. His practice of walking about while teaching resulted in the so-called Peripatetic School. Although I have found walking about to be the best way to get my thoughts moving, I am not an Aristotelian. Going for a morning walk is simply an excellent way of beginning one's day and getting one's body and soul wide awake.

I am curious by nature, and I have worked out the pace of walking that suits me best. If I go too fast, all my energy goes into the physical performance, which is sometimes nice and relaxing. After all, we are "animals" who enjoy moving and playing around. A brisk walk loosens up tensions and drives away disturbing thoughts. As we increase our speed they are wiped out of our minds. It is a matter of fact that we cannot have more than one thought in our mind at the same time. The quickest way to get rid of those that bother us, then, is to focus on the physical existence of our body, or to allow ourselves to be completely absorbed in what we are doing. This is what Carl Gustav Jung (d. 1961) learned in his practice of analytical psychology.

Too slow a pace, on the other hand, allows your thoughts to wander around like monkeys in a zoo. The scenery may draw your attention, then nature, the scent of flowers and other objects of interest in the environment. This is quite nice occasionally. Who would not enjoy being out in the open, admiring the blooming of the various flowers? Being a nature lover myself, I find it soothing that the flowers that fade away in the late autumn are mocking death by springing up again in the spring. The seasons of nature encourage me to rely on the inherent energy of creativity. As flowers blossom, so in every human being there is a well of healing energy. It is therefore of vital importance to be in continuous touch with that life-maintaining well.

To clear one's thoughts, then, presupposes a walking rhythm, neither too brisk nor too lingering. If the idea is to attain a focused state in order to solve some problem or find the right words with which to express one's ideas, the walking has to proceed more slowly. Thus I start off at a rather brisk pace to really wake up my body after the night's rest. When the pulse is somewhat accelerated, the body becomes warm and the muscles flexible. To get rid of the morning stiffness, both body and soul have to reach a certain temperature. As soon as my thoughts begin to move I slow down, because my aim is not to get back home as quickly as possible, but to follow the movements of my mind.

On my morning walks I always focus on one question I am trying to resolve, and do my best to keep my mind fixed on one issue only. Whenever I need to write a column for a newspaper, a reference, or a scholarly essay, I allow my thoughts to ponder on the subject as freely as possible during the physical exercise. To my own surprise, I have noticed how perfectly the peripatetic technique works. As I return home, I often have most of the words already in my head, and it is only a matter of saving them in my PC. The final draft requires some re-reading and correcting, of course, but the hardest part has been engraved in my memory during that refreshing walk.

When, years ago, I took up this habit, dedicated joggers advised me to run instead of walk. At first I experienced some feeling of inferiority, but that totally disappeared as I came across a book on ancient Chinese philosophy on one of my sojourns in the library. There it was clearly stated that hurrying and running are unhealthy. According to the ancient Chinese, physical exercise, like making love, should be performed in such a way that sweat never starts to flow. Insofar as we start to sweat, we have already overdone it, and that is against the basic principles of *tao*, the harmony that keeps the balance and maintains life. Peter Nansen's (d. 1918) advice seems appropriate here: "It is no use running if it is in the wrong direction."

2

I AM ALONE ON THE BEACH. Christos was right. The beach is mine. There has been nobody but me on the seashore the whole day. There was no need for a bathing suit. My third day in Ouranoupolis has passed like the others: walking around, writing in my diary, sunbathing before taking a light lunch of Greek salad, swimming and resting on the beach the whole afternoon until sunset.

During my first visit to Ouranoupolis in 1984, the wife of the house in which I was staying came to clean my room as I was sunbathing on the balcony. "*Iliotherapeía*," she stated as she caught me completely by surprise. "Sun therapy!" What a wonderful word for sunbathing, I immediately thought. For many years I have used it to justify being lazy in the sun. I have convinced my friends, and also myself, that it is a form of therapy. "I'll go for my therapy session," I then used to say to the staff in my office in the afternoon when I went to sit for a while on the steps of the main Cathedral in Helsinki, a place that fills with students and tourists as soon as the first sun shows itself in the spring. The steps facing south are an ideal place for "sun therapy."

Years later I realized that what I enjoyed in my "sun therapy" was not only the sun, but above all the fact that as soon as I allowed the rays of the sun to warm up my body, the stress disappeared and my mind became relaxed. That was what I longed for at stressful times long before the word came into common parlance. However, as Freud and certainly many before him also noticed, I discovered that as soon as I was relaxed, thoughts came into my mind, jumping around like squirrels—conflicts at work, things I had forgotten to do, ideas for scholarly articles. The relaxed moment turned instantly into one of strain as thoughts began to bother me. Sometimes they hang around for a long time, but often they go away as unexpectedly as they come and new things come to mind. What for years has been a "bad habit" of mine is now called quality time, though it refers more to the time we spend developing our relationships with members of our family than to the time we reserve for learning to understand ourselves.

Since the very beginning of my university career, I have kept Thursdays as my personal holiday of the week. Being a Finland-Swede, I thought it appropriate to celebrate *Thors dag* as my day off from the university, the day of the Scandinavian god Thor, the fifth day of the week known as the day of thunder, Thursday. This day, when the god Thor put all chaotic things into order, was as good a day as any to spend reading and writing, in other words on my research.

The first time I used this excuse I did so more or less as a joke. I told the Dean of the Department of Theology that unfortunately I could not come to a meeting on Thursday because it was the day I celebrated Thor. I would not go to the university on a Thursday even if it were a matter of life and death. However—if resurrection were at hand, I could bend my principles a little. Then she laughed and said that the meeting would not be that serious. Since then, what started out as a witticism became a habit, and only seldom have I taken part in any event at the university on a Thursday.

Thursdays are completely reserved for research, or as I understand it, for wondering about things that have to do with being-in-this-world, especially religious issues. Who am I? Who are my neighbors? How do they conceive of being in the world and of religious spirituality? How have people through the ages expressed themselves regarding these questions? The following Irish prayer made me realize how important it is to seize the moment.

> Give yourself enough time:
> to work—it is the price of success;
> to think—it is the well of power;
> to play—it is the secret of eternal youth;

to read—it is the foundation of wisdom;
to be polite—it is the path to happiness;
to dream—it is to join the stars;
to love and be loved—it is the privilege of the
      gods;
to look around—there is no time for narrowness;
to laugh—it is the music of the soul.

Thus I nearly always stay home on Thursdays. Every now and then, of course, it is beneficial to deviate from one's habits. Sometimes chaos is a welcome guest in the midst of order. With this in mind, as I was on my way to the library I stopped off at my office to get a book and a letter to the heads of departments caught my eye. I opened it and was extremely surprised when I read that I should encourage my staff to take part in a two-day seminar outside of Helsinki to discuss how to reform the system for reserving lecture rooms. I could not believe my eyes. A two-day seminar on how to reserve lecture rooms! The university administration wants to put everything on computer to smooth the routines. That I can accept, but organizing a seminar for it is madness. Do they really want staff from all departments to spend two days learning how to book their lecture rooms? They cannot have thought this through. Do they want professors, whose education has largely been paid for by the state, and who after years of studying and research are now the most learned people in our society, to waste their time on this kind of bureaucracy? I was amazed and perplexed.

Professors are usually more than forty years of age when they get their chair. At best they have about twenty-five years left to study and teach in the departments before retirement. Every day they spend away from research and teaching, which after all should be their main duty, by taking part in meetings and seminars organized by the administration is a day taken away from what they are supposed to be doing. Their days are numbered. Why does the administration not do everything in its power to keep us occupied with our main tasks? That would be highly appreciated.

Nowadays, hours and days are wasted in writing reports about how we spend our time, about departmental finances and policy, reports of the year that has passed and strategies for the future. There is no end to the time-consuming bureaucracy, which has grown out of all proportion over the last twenty years. This is a total misuse of the potential of the most educated scholars and scientists in the country.

University teachers are world champions in their own subjects. What do you think the British people would say if the best of their athletes, after having trained for years, were to sit around a table and spend days thinking about how best to book arenas? There is no end to stupidity!

This letter made me so upset that, without the slightest hesitation, I let my anarchist tendencies loose. I made a model airplane of the form, as we sometimes used to do during our school days, opened the window and threw it out into the air. Freedom! Take it whoever wants it!

I do not think that taxpayers, who in their own way have contributed to my education, will blame me for that. More determined than ever, I left my office and headed for the library. I have been trained to do research and that, by God, is my priority above all. When I have achieved some results, then I will happily share what I have found, not only with my students at the university, but also with the general public in the form of lectures, speeches, interviews in the media and by writing books. In Finland, the main task of university professors is to study and then to teach what they have found to be the "truth" on the basis of their first-hand research.

Recently my eyes caught an article in the university newsletter, reporting how some "genius" had created a so-called research-based teaching model. Again, I could not believe my eyes. It was presented as the central strategy of our university teaching to narrow the gap between teachers and students. I was perplexed. Since 1975, when I began teaching at the university, I have always taught what I have learned during my field experiences and research, first in Sri Lanka among Buddhist monks and laymen, and then in Greece among Orthodox monks and pilgrims. How, then, can the research-based teaching model be something new? My own teachers primarily taught what they had studied first-hand themselves. The memory really is short.

It is obvious that the teaching at the university should always be based on recent research. As far as I know, this has been the case since time immemorial. The task of a teacher is to be inspiring and to provoke questions and answers, a dialogue with the students, so that the phenomenon of understanding may take place. There is nothing new about that. It is merely the so-called administrative planners at the university who are new, naive and obsessed with political agendas. The main aim seems to be reform, even when it is of no use or when a good working system is destroyed. I am not too optimistic about the recent developments at universities in Europe. Will Bologna save us? I doubt it.

When I sat down in the library I immediately began to work furiously on my entry on pilgrimage. I was desperate to finish it before starting my journey. Before I left I wandered among the shelves merely to enjoy the silence. By accident my hands reached out for an old book, the spine beautifully decorated in golden lettering. It was the book in which I found the aforementioned lithograph by Vincenzo Coronelli. A strange coincidence, I reflected.

Being familiar with the Buddhist way of thinking, I first thought that the whole thing was insignificant. In Buddhism events are merely events, and it is what we attach to them that makes them something more. If we do not crave them, there is no suffering, because suffering is the result of craving, longing and wanting things. On the other hand, what makes life interesting is precisely the fact that, for the time being, in an inexplicable way events are not merely events, but are somehow connected. Carl Gustav Jung called this *synchronicity*, the "acausal connecting principle" that creates meaningful inner relationships among external events occurring at the same time.

It is indeed a strange coincidence that the day before I left once again for Ouranoupolis, I re-discovered the book with a lithograph of a monastic island that enthralled me to the extent that I felt compelled to visit that island. It was no coincidence, as

Jung surely would have argued, but an invitation I should accept, because it had to do with my individuation, the growing of my inner self.

Christos comes back from the monastery of Dionysiou tomorrow. I feel restless. I am so eager to visit the island. I am already tired of lying on the beach, allowing thoughts to be reflected in my mind, thinking about the entry, the drudgery at the university and all the other bothersome thoughts that appear as I am doing nothing. I now need some action. The worst thing that could happen would be that I would suddenly come upon something I should have included in my entry, but forgot to put there as I hurried to finish my work.

Therefore, in my mind I try to climb the tower, and look at the sea from the balcony. I look out for the island, although I know it is not nearby. I can see it in my imagination, or rather the lithographic impression brings it to my mind. It is strange how convinced I am that the monastic island does exist. It is equally odd that I strongly believe that Christos knows its whereabouts. Tomorrow I will know for sure.

PART TWO

Divina Laterna

The Monastic Island

"Am I too early?"

"No, not at all, Renéos," Christos said. "Let's fry some fish and have a glass of the very best Athos wine." For him everything that came from the Holy Mountain was the best of its kind.

"*Mávro krasí, parakaló!*"

"I know, Renéos, you like red wine more than retsina," he said with a smile.

"Yes. The Athos wine is the best."

"I agree. It's the best."

Christos had recently married. He had one son. His wife and son spend most of the day in his mother's house, so there were only the two of us. This was a blessing, because I could have his undivided attention, and could ask him about the location of the monastic island and how to get there. When the family is around he is always being interrupted either by his wife or his son. This is natural, but a nuisance for me. It is also stressful for him. He cannot commit himself to all three of us at the same time. He becomes restless. The typical Greek custom of whiling away the day in good conversation on the uncomfortable traditional blue chairs is impossible to maintain.

Christos has devoted his life to serving the Athonites. Consequently he spends his days fixing all kinds of mechanical equipment used in the monasteries, from servicing outboard motor engines, power saws and pickups or jeeps to installing solar panels and helping with the gardening. His benevolence often results in long working hours. Hence he hardly ever keeps to a schedule. For him time does not exist in the Western sense of the term.

Days pass. The expressions morning, afternoon and evening are flexible to the point of becoming meaningless in terms of any kind of exactness. "See you in the morning," may mean anything from nine to one o'clock and "See you in the afternoon," suggests anything between one o'clock and six or even seven in the evening, usually until sunset.

Knowing this, I was not too surprised that it took more than an hour before lunch was ready. It is a Greek habit to invite friends for lunch or supper and to start cooking only after everyone has arrived. This may have something to do with the fact that nobody keeps the time and you can never be sure that people will actually turn up. Anyway, before the plates are put on the table, all the ingredients have to be found, the fish fried, and… and, inevitably, more than an hour has passed. Although I am familiar with this rhythm, I still always feel surprised and impatient during my first days in Ouranoupolis. Don't get me wrong. I very much appreciate being invited for supper. It is only that I am usually starving by the time I get to the table. However, it has always proved worth the wait. This time, too, the fish were delicious and the Athos wine superb. Eventually the wine loosened my tongue. I could not avoid confessing to Christos the real purpose of my sojourn.

"Christos," I said hesitantly, "I've heard that there's an island nearby. It's like a huge meteorite that landed in the middle of the sea. The edges of the cliffs rise steeply for more than twenty meters. It's impossible to climb to its plateau. Nonetheless, a hermit is said to live on the plateau, a spiritual father of exceptional wisdom. Do you know where this island is?"

"How did you hear about this island?"

"Accidently. I came across a lithograph in an old book. It was impressive. I even dreamt of it the next night. I was taking turns praying '*Kyrie, eleison*' with the hermit living in the *kellion*."

"Strange. Only very few know about it. The hermit doesn't want visitors. It's impossible to climb the cliffs."

"Do you know its whereabouts?" I asked again.

"Of course. I take food to him once a week. He's a cousin of mine, but, as I told you, he doesn't want to be disturbed."

"*Málista* (yes), I understand. The flow of pilgrims to the Holy Mountain is really stressful for the monks."

"He wants to devote himself to his spiritual struggle. He moved to the island to assist an old monk who could no longer live alone. When the monk died, he decided to stay there as a hermit."

"I'd like to come with you when you take food to him the next time," I said, as casually as I could.

"That's not possible. I've promised not to tell anyone about the island and not to take anyone with me when I visit him."

"But Christos, can't you explain to him that I saw him in my dreams? Tell him that because of that prophetic dream I'm now here to meet him."

Christos pretended not to listen to my Orthodox argument. I continued to press him. I simply had to visit the island.

"Christos, the monastic island that I saw in my dreams really exists. It must surely be a divine message to me, urging me to visit it."

"I'll be going to the island tomorrow," he revealed, as if unintentionally.

"Can't you call him and tell him my story?"

"I suppose I could call him," he said hesitantly.

"Please, do!"

"He has a mobile phone these days. The storm last autumn nearly killed him, as he had to wait for help for more than a week."

"Can't you call him now? Please!" I persisted with my request. "He's most likely to be in his *kellion* at this time of the day. It's too hot to work in the garden. He's probably resting after his meal, as we are. Please, it would mean so much to me," I pleaded with him once more.

A little perplexed, he eventually made the telephone call. Nearly everyone in the village has a Nokia mobile phone for reasons of safety, especially when fishing at sea. The teenagers, of course, have their own, but the older generation also seem to be carrying them this year. They are the hit of the season. Wherever you go you can hear the familiar call sounds in the distance.

"I'm much obliged to you for your help." I expressed my gratitude to Christos as I could see how reluctant he was to make the call. His response was to lift his head high with a stiff upper lip, as the Greeks always do when they disagree, sometimes murmuring *óhi* (no). Now the gesture was his silent protest against my pressuring him.

It took some time before the hermit answered. Christos spoke at such a speed that I found it difficult to understand what he said. The longer they talked, the more worried I became. I crossed myself out of nervousness as the conversation continued. Later I found out that Christos had some explaining to do, and that he was working hard to convince the hermit that my intentions were honourable. He called him *géronda*, which literally means "old man," but in the Athonite context refers to a senior monk or hermit venerated as a spiritual counsellor and father. He introduced me to the hermit as his Finnish friend, who had visited the Holy Mountain annually since 1984 and who now wanted to deepen his spiritual life. When, after an exchange of many words that I did not catch, he finally said *málista* (yes), I concluded that the outcome was positive. Somewhat embarrassed but somehow satisfied, he told me that I could go with him the next day.

"Splendid!" I exclaimed in delight. "I'm really grateful to you for your help."

"We've to leave before dawn," Christos replied laconically. "The voyage is long."

"At what time shall we meet?" I asked, to be sure to be in time. There was no way I was going to miss this chance, which I suspected would be a major turning point in my life. I had reached middle-age and perhaps was also facing a mid-life crisis. In any case, I was convinced that my outer and inner lives were going to meet on the monastic island. I was in a state that resembled an erupting volcano, having reached the point of no return. I could only guess what consequences this was going to have for me. My whole body and soul were full of expectation.

"Come to my boat at five o'clock," Christos said. "You remember where I keep it?"

"I remember."

Christos offered me another glass of wine. I welcomed it in my state of excitement. We talked about this and that. I did not really pay much attention to what he said and cannot recall any details. In my mind I was already on the monastic island. It existed. It was hard to believe the whole story was really true. Christos had some preparations to make before the journey, so after once again expressing my sincere thanks, I went in a state of euphoria to the beach, had a swim, and lay down to rest.

2

IT WAS ALREADY FOUR O'CLOCK, but the sun was still warm. There was no one else on the beach. It was just as well, because I wanted to prepare myself for tomorrow's journey. It is rather a poor plan for everyone to take their holiday at the same time of the year. The prices are higher and the best-loved places are crowded. The weather here is still excellent in late autumn, and the prices are more favorable. This is perfect for those who are retired and are not bound to any schedule other than their own health. It is usually pleasant in Greece until the beginning of November, sometimes even later, although the mornings and evenings are chilly. The sea is warm until the stormy winds hit the coasts and bring cold water into the bays.

I lingered until sunset by the big stone at the end of the beach. This side of the beach is full of pebbles, but there is a soft sandy path to the sea. Every spring the locals clean the path, which the winter storms tend to refill with pebbles. Apart from being slippery, they also have sharp edges thanks to the shells attached to them. It is not entirely without risk to go into the water stepping on these stones. Once I got a rather nasty cut on my toe and it took some time to heal. I did not want to take any chances this time, so I stuck to the path.

I felt like Robinson Crusoe as I undressed and went naked to swim. The water was warm. I could stay for quite some time relaxing in the sea, allowing myself to be carried to the shore by the waves. The clear blue water, the lapping of the waves and the sweet autumn wind drying my skin after the swim made me feel as if I were in heaven. It was most enjoyable: not too hot, not too windy, no worries, only the excitement of waiting filled my mind, like when I was a child waiting for Father Christmas. All my wishes could still come true. This air of expectancy is perhaps the best state in our life. As soon as we get our presents, disappointment also creeps in. Not all of the gifts meet our expectations.

The glittering sea brings new images from my past. My life is projected on my visual memory like impressionist snapshots. The series of moving pictures goes back and forth, as it has done during these last few days. My life and career are clearly depicted in front of my inner eyes until I realize that I am once more looking at the tower: *Memento mori!* Remember that you are mortal! How am I to proceed from here?

It seems so trivial to say that I am in the midst of a mid-life crisis. It is so common and trendy. It is in fact ridiculous, but nevertheless true. I feel the pinch. I have reached what there is to be reached. I have climbed the career ladder to the very top. Still, I am dissatisfied. I do not feel comfortable. Although I can see far, in the long run it is boring up here. At times it is also quite windy, lonely and unrewarding. After all, there are other mountains, too. At the top there are too many things I feel I have to take into consideration. There are expectations and obligations. There is far too little time to use all the experiences and knowledge I have gathered over the years. I have reached the point in my career where I am no longer interested in performing the duties and tasks assigned to me. Work now seems to occupy too much of my precious time. It is frustrating to have to deal with matters that are of no "real" concern. Bureaucracy may have a function, but none whatsoever from the viewpoint of research, and especially of my private spiritual progress. I feel alienated from the world in which I live. The university world is so full of things that do not really matter. The question, "Who am I?" occupies me more than, "Am I fulfilling my duties?" There is no denying that I now find myself at a crossroads in my life, as did Hercules, who had to choose between the path of virtue and that of desire.

Perhaps I should regard my present feelings as meaning that life is calling me to take on new kinds of assignments, not dictated by the expectations of my parents or anyone else, but given by life itself, the innermost part of my being. When I listen to these words as they pop up from my subconscious the very moment I jot them down in my diary, I feel inspired. There is still something alive inside me that wants to clothe itself in words. The revitalization is so compelling that it urges me to continue on the inner path. I am like a pilgrim in the Middle Ages, who does not know the difficulties ahead, but who, despite the uncertainty, realizes that the pilgrimage has to be completed. It is an inner calling that cannot be ignored unless one wants to wither like a plant out of water. The spiritual well once found has to be used before one can go on with one's life.

Worldly affairs and worries seem insignificant compared to the delight of the inner world. What do people think of me? Am I behaving according to expectations? Am I successful in other people's eyes? Years ago these questions seemed important and caused me many unnecessary worries. In mid-life they seem irrelevant. Who cares!

Greeks are more spontaneous than Finns in many respects. They also have a healthy self-esteem, sometimes perhaps even a little too healthy. Proud as they are of their history, especially the time of Alexander the Great and the Byzantine epoch, they occasionally fall into *uppishness* and vanity. They need to show off to their neighbors how well they are doing economically, for example, because money is often an issue, and the most important one in the race for success.

This can be seen in the evenings after sunset when Ouranoupolitan families walk up and down the asphalt main road and the street by the row of *tavernas*. They talk to one another as they go by on their way to visit friends, or simply stroll around having a nice time, sometimes ending up at one of the *tavernas* for a light evening meal or just a drink.

Everyone is well dressed, especially the children, who wear their best clothes. It is no exaggeration when I say that the evening is, in many respects, the high point of the day, at least regarding the social life in the village. Even the men tend to dress up a little, or at least they put on clean trousers and a fancy shirt. Apart from the locals, there are only a few pilgrims and visitors on their way to the Holy Mountain.

As in other Mediterranean countries, social life begins after sunset and lasts until midnight, when the *tavernas* close for the day, although a few stay open as long as they have customers. Once, I recall, we went for supper at one o'clock in the morning. This time of the year the locals prefer to go to bed a little earlier as many of them feel exhausted after the long tourist season. Nevertheless, you can hear the unmarried men chatting late at night with a glass of beer or ouzo to keep the discussion going.

As I walked to my room late in the evening, the silence of the winter was already perceptible. I am not so sure I could live here through the winter, although I have often thought it would be an interesting adventure. It would not be difficult to find peace to write, but the loneliness and the absence of a library with all the new books would certainly be impossible to cope with in the long run. Or perhaps not. Each of us is a living library, full of experiences, which, through conversation, can be read, understood and learned from. Still, I could not live without my books. Sooner or later I would get tired of listening to peoples' stories, which tend to be the same or mostly quite trivial to those of us who are not questioning anthropologists. There is no end of books, and the verbal expressions used are so full of nuances that I always find myself fascinated by the richness of language.

3

"KALIMÉRA (GOOD MORNING), Christos."
"*Kaliméra*, Renéos. I'm sorry I'm late."
"*Típota* (It doesn't matter)."
"I had so many things to take to the *géronda*. He called me late in the evening and asked me to bring the power saw, too."

"Are there trees on the island?" I was a little surprised.

"Not many. The storm last winter uprooted the biggest and oldest one. Autumn is already well on its way. The tree has to be chopped up for firewood before the rain comes."

"The winter seems to be hard on the island."

"Some years ago the *géronda* even had snow in his garden. I've also got a warm coat for you. The wind can be unfriendly before sunrise."

The early mornings are really cold. I was grateful to Christos for his thoughtfulness. I was not prepared for a long voyage, so I had not packed a windbreaker. A sweater, though warm, is not enough protection against the wind.

"How long is the voyage?" I asked when we were sitting in the boat and Christos was about to start the engine.

"It'll take about five hours. We have to stay there overnight."

"That's fine by me," I replied, satisfied with the turn of events. I wanted nothing more than to stay with the hermit.

There was no one on the shore as we prepared for departure. The only sign of life was the flashing light from the little lighthouse at the end of the concrete jetty. It cheerily wished us *bon voyage* as we slowly headed out into the darkness. As we drew further away from the shore, Ouranoupolis became a fringe of lights with the flashing lighthouse in the middle. From October onwards the tranquil village life is interrupted only twice a day: in the morning at about half past nine and in the afternoon around half past one, when the port is crowded with men, both pilgrims and visitors. They arrive in the morning by bus from Thessalonica to catch the 9:45 ferry to Daphne, the main port on the Holy Mountain. As soon as the pilgrims have stepped down onto the asphalt they rush up the main road to the Pilgrims' Office to get their *diamonitírion* (visa), which allows them to stay eight days on the Holy Mountain. They form a disorderly queue and eventually get their permits. Then one by one they hurry down to the *taverna* by the jetty for refreshments. The three-hour ride early in the morning is somewhat tiring and everyone is in need of Greek coffee and a slice of spinach or cheese pie. Then they fill up their rucksacks or bags with biscuits, water and cigarettes from one of the kiosks, and finally, with an expectant gaze in their eyes, they walk along the long jetty to board the ferry.

Once the ferry has departed, life in the village returns to normal until half past one in the afternoon. First, ships from the other peninsulas bring tourists for a few hours' visit to Ouranoupolis, and then when the Athos ferry returns with pilgrims from Daphne the reverse procedure takes place. The bus is already waiting by the tower to take them back to Thessalonica, tired but content.

Apart from these two rush hours, life is usually nice and tranquil. The only noises to be heard are the roosters that wake you up at dawn, the owls' "whoo-whoo's" and the cutting of wood for the winter, first with huge power saws and then manually with axes. Today the villagers live for five or so months of the year on tourism, usually from Easter until late September, and the rest on fishing, agriculture, gardening, handicrafts and various kinds of seasonal and temporary work on the Holy Mountain—olive picking, hunting and so on.

The old men are to be seen sitting on the traditional basket chairs outside their *tavernas* or houses, discussing, playing chess or cards, throwing dice, walking up and down the main street, playing with their keys or with prayer beads. The women often sit in smaller groups, knitting and gossiping about the latest news in the village. The younger people move to the bigger cities for the winter, either to study or to work. Many of them even manage to get temporary employment in Germany, where they go for a year or so mainly to earn money, buy a car and bring some money back to the family. The children attend the village primary school. Of the six hundred villagers, only a few hundred remain there throughout the year.

The port is the heart of Ouranoupolis. It is a safe haven for the fishermen and their boats. After hours on the stormy sea they are relieved to find shelter from the big waves behind the breakwater. The extended jetty jutting out far into the Aegean Sea is not only a shelter for sailors and fishermen. It is also a port of departure for the adventurous. Many have stood on it and looked out to sea, feeling an intense longing to journey into the unknown. Some have defied the raging waters only to return humiliated by the force that swallowed their best friend. When calm the sea is sweet, but it is brutal when stormy.

The shrine of St. Nicholas, the protector of the seafarer, is at the other end of the port. There is always a light burning there in commemoration of those who have been lost at sea, and also warning against the biggest danger of all, namely the luring hubris that blurs our judgement. As our boat drew further from the shore I could see the tiny light in the shrine urging me to be careful. Christos told me years ago that an old widow lights it first thing in the morning and immediately after sunset in memory of her husband, who was swallowed by the storm, and as a prayer for his soul.

Every port is a bridge to another harbour. In the case of the ports at Ouranoupolis and Daphne, this bridge connects the monastic and the secular worlds, the sacred and the profane. All the ferries to the monasteries of the Holy Mountain depart from Ouranoupolis, and only some smaller boats leave from the village of Ierissos on the other side of the peninsula. The border between the sacred and the secular is never as clearly perceived as when you return from the Holy Mountain to the bay of Ouranoupolis. "Women!" is the immediate cry. There are no women on the Holy Mountain. During the eight days you are there you are so absorbed by the monastic atmosphere that you do not even think about them. When you return to the real world, the contrast is glaring as the wives and girlfriends of the pilgrims wait for their loved ones on the jetty, waving to them in welcome dressed only in their tiny bikinis. It is a shock to any normal man, and I cannot even begin to imagine what the monks must think about it. As in paradise, a leaf is surely missing!

The engine was so loud that there was no point talking to Christos during the voyage. He was sitting at the back steering, and I was curled up down in the front taking shelter from the wind. Every now and then he nodded to make sure that I was okay. We had already left the Holy Mountain behind us and it was completely out of sight when he pointed to the right-hand side of the boat. With an air of expectancy I immediately looked out to sea. At least a dozen dolphins were swimming parallel to our boat, slowly coming nearer and nearer. In no time we were completely surrounded by a joyful shoal, who entertained us for quite a while as if they themselves enjoyed our company. They jumped up high in the air and then down again, some of them swimming so close to our boat that I could have touched their backs had I dared to. The sun was already up and it was as if the dolphins had come to pilot us to the monastic island. I felt light-hearted and became more convinced than ever that there was a predestined meaning in my going there.

The dolphins swam alongside our boat for at least half an hour, possibly more. Their joyful playing was a good break in the monotonous journey. Five hours on the sea is quite some time. Although the sun had already warmed our bodies, the sitting made us stiff and I tried to move around as much as I could.

The dolphins were long gone and I had apparently had a catnap when Christos shouted at me to turn around. The sea was still very calm, and at first I only looked down into the water, following how the boat's bow was gently carving a path through it. Then he shouted again, urging me to look up. I did so and could not believe my eyes. Straight ahead of us was a high and steep cliff. It was as if a huge cruise liner was approaching. The majestic cliff looked formidable—I was still drowsy from both the sleep and the sun. Christos slowed down. Our boat was gliding smoothly along the rocky wall. The closer we came, the steeper it turned out to be. At one point I was overcome by fear when I wondered how on earth I would be able to climb up to the plateau where the hermit lived, safe from intruders. There was no path and no steps. Wide with surprise, my eyes focused the cliffs as I tried desperately to find some clue as to how we were to land on the island. Christos steered the boat slowly along the rock face until suddenly he turned it straight into a tiny cave carved out by the sea. As we entered the cave he stopped the engine and the boat glided silently into the darkness.

"*Eulogíte* (Be blessed)," Christos said as our boat entered the cave.

"*O Kyrios,*" a voice replied from inside. It took some time before my eyes became used to the darkness, as we had spent more than four hours in the sun and glittering waters. Gradually I recognized the figure of a hermit standing on the narrow jetty on the left side of our boat as the bluish-green light from the water was reflected in his tanned face, which was full of vivacity in contrast to his long black monastic dress, *ráson*, and soft black cap, *skouphos*.

"*Eulogíte,*" I echoed out of courtesy.

"*O Kyrios,*" the hermit repeated.

The hermit skillfully tied the mooring rope to the two metal rings on the jetty. Then we loaded all our things into a wheelbarrow. When that was done, the hermit began to walk slowly along a narrow path into the cave. Christos pushed the wheelbarrow behind him and I followed in their footsteps. After a few minutes the narrow passage widened into a glade lit by sunlight from above. In the middle of the cliff there was a wide crack going straight into the bottom of the cave. When my eyes became used to the bright sunlight peeping in from the clear blue sky, I saw a lift in front of us, built against the wall of the rock. For years the lift had functioned only manually, but some years ago Christos had managed to make it work by means of electricity from the solar panels. The power was only enough for one person at a time. Therefore it took quite some time before all of us and the wheelbarrow were safely on the plateau, which seemed to be about four floors up from the level of the cave. The lift rose extremely slowly. At one point I began to wonder if it still had enough power in it to take me to the top, as I was the last one to use it. I felt relieved when I finally stood on the plateau and Christos introduced me properly to the hermit.

"My friend here's from Finland. He's a professor at the University of Helsinki. A few weeks ago he dreamt about this island and felt an urge to visit it."

The hermit listened attentively. Then he asked what my name was. Before Christos answered I said:

"René."

"*Málista* (Good)," he said, "*málista. René* means "born again" from the Latin word *renatus*," he explained. "*Málista*," he repeated once more as if he was pondering about my name.

I was extremely surprised that the hermit knew the etymology of my name. Few write it correctly, as I mentioned earlier, and even fewer know its etymology. It was obvious that, apart from being a virtuoso in spiritual matters, he also was a man of learning.

Knowing that the voyage to the island is tiring, the hermit led us immediately to his monastic cottage, in Greek generally known as a *kellion*. Christos pushed the wheelbarrow the fifty meters from the lift to the house and left it there in the shade. We emptied it of the food and water, which we put into the fridge in the kitchen. Then, in accordance with the custom on the Holy Mountain, the hermit first took us to the small chapel at the end of the house. As we entered it he told us that it was dedicated to St. Nicholas. He crossed himself as we stepped into the nave and then went straight to the icon of St. Nicholas, crossed himself again, kissed it, and made the sign of the cross once more. Christos did the same and so did I. I kissed the icon with great relief and comfort. The voyage here had been safe.

As we stood in front of St. Nicholas, the hermit whispered its story: "At the time of the iconoclastic heresy this icon was struck by a heretic monk, who then threw it into the sea. In 1593, now more than four hundred years ago, a fisherman brought it up in his net. There was an oyster stuck to the forehead on the spot where the heretic had struck St. Nicholas. When the fisherman removed the oyster, blood poured from the wounds, the blood of Christ, the fisherman thought. Horrified by the miracle he quickly brought it to the chapel, where is has been kept ever since."

Christos quickly kissed the miraculous icon in mosaic once more, and so did I, grateful that he had protected us on our voyage.

After a few minutes of prayer in the chapel, the hermit took us to the kitchen where he had prepared some food for us. After grace, he poured us some red wine, wishing us welcome to his humble house. We crossed ourselves and quickly began to eat the minestrone soup, dipping the hard pieces of bread into it to dissolve them. In addition to the bread, we all had a huge tomato, black olives, a piece of halvah and grapes for desert. The soup was tepid, but necessary to break up the hard bread. There was next to no discussion while we were eating. Christos and I were hungry and tired. The hermit offered us more soup and bread, and looked kindly at me. This made me feel comfortable and at home in the strange environment.

When we had eaten, the hermit showed us into his living room and then advised us to rest, as indeed he was also going to do. The sun was already at its zenith. It was far too hot to work outside. Christos lay down on the sofa that lined the wall, as I am sure he must have done hundreds of times before, tired by the fresh air at sea and the voyage. He was due to chop up the tree in the late afternoon so he needed some rest. With a peaceful mind I followed his example and lay down at the other end of the sofa. Before falling asleep I heard Christos snoring now and again, but exhausted by the long journey and the experiences of the day, I soon dozed off.

4

I WOKE UP TWO HOURS LATER to the sound of the power saw. Christos was already chopping up the tree. From the window I could see the hermit giving him a hand. Embarrassed, I hurried out to help them in their work. The tree was completely dry. Christos cut the trunk and the larger branches into two-foot pieces, while the hermit and I split the thicker parts in two with axes. Then we moved them by wheelbarrow to the house and stacked them against the wall under cover. The work was quickly done. In gratitude the hermit took me to a huge grapevine and gave me a large bunch of grapes.

"*Euvlogíae* (Blessings)," I said spontaneously.

"Quite right, Renéos, these are blessings for a hermit." He was in a good mood.

The cheerful and unreserved character of the hermit encouraged me to ask him his name, since I realized with surprise that Christos had never told me. On the telephone and here he always called him *géronda*.

"*Géronda*," I began hesitantly. "May I ask you what your name is?"

"Theophilos," he said immediately, "Theophilos."

Christos, overhearing our discussion, came to the vine and explained that *Theophilos* meant "loved by God." Then he praised Father Theophilos as the most spiritual monk of all the Athonites. This troubled the hermit, who immediately corrected him.

"In spiritual matters no one is better than anyone else. Athonites are working hard to please God and to follow his will. It's a long journey. No one can lay down to rest before he's in his grave. Falling is always only a second away. "Be on your guard!" he shouted at Christos."

Father Theophilos then showed us his olive trees and his vegetable garden, where he had onions and tomatoes. He told us that fertile soil had been brought to him by an army helicopter in recent years. A relative of his is in the army and as they fly over to guard the Turkish border they usually bring him bags of soil and other things he needs to survive. The clefts in the rock have been widened into large water basins with many channels carrying water from the slopes of the mountain. Life is trying on the island, but not impossible given good planning. The lack of water is the most difficult problem, but there is usually enough rain for the bare necessities. "Blessings from God," Father Theophilos calls both the rain and the vegetables, as well as the fish he gets from the sea. His garden struggles for survival as he struggles spiritually for the mercy of God.

The plateau is about 50 meters wide and 100 meters long. It resembles an atrium in that it is between sheltering cliffs rising straight up, high into the sky. Only the front side is open to the sea. It seems like the garden of Eden, at least to me, although there is, of course, no picture in the Bible of the first garden of humankind.

After Father Theophilos had shown us the plateau, we went into his house, and in no time he brought a tray into the living room with glasses of water, *raki*, Greek coffee and pieces of *loukoumi*, the way pilgrims are welcomed on the Holy Mountain. Accustomed as I was to the Athonite tradition, I immediately drank the *raki*—a spirit strong as vodka—straight down, ate the *loukoumi*, a Turkish delight, drank the water and started slowly to sip the coffee while listening to the discussion between Christos and Father Theophilos.

Christos speaks Greek very quickly as do many Ouranoupolitans. I am not sure if it is a kind of dialect of those who migrated from Asia Minor, or if there are other reasons for the villagers' habit of abbreviating words, but the fact remains that it is sometimes quite difficult to follow. Father Theophilos, on the other hand, spoke slowly and deliberately, pondering a while after each word. I soon understood that they were talking about the shortage of water. The reservoirs were nearly empty as there had been no rain for several months. The garden badly needed water. Christos promised to contact their friend in the army and ask him to bring some water on his next flight through that area. Some of the helicopters carry loads of water with them to extinguish the fires that occasionally flare up unexpectedly for no apparent reason. Greece suffers many fires every summer, and the Holy Mountain is no exception.

Father Theophilos had no shortage of food. He had been fishing three days in a row and caught plenty in his net. With the vegetables, bread and grapes we brought him he said he could feed an army. Having said that, he turned round and asked me: "Did you say you wanted to stay here for the week?"

"I'd be delighted," I replied, quite surprised by his offer. This is what I had hoped for, but had not dared to ask him yet. At that moment I could easily have promised to stay a month or two, if that had been an option. I was so sure that my sojourn on the island would be not only enlightening, but above all life-affirming. I noticed that Christos was also quite astounded by the hospitality of Father Theophilos.

"When is your flight back home?" Christos asked.

"I have an open ticket," I said, showing my relief. As it happened, I was not in an hurry. I only wanted to follow my dream. That was the main purpose of my being-in-this-world.

"Then it's settled," Father Theophilos concluded. "Christos will be back next week, God willing. You can go back with him then. This island is austere, but there is much work to be done, especially in spiritual matters." He made the sign of the cross thus blessing my decision to take up my spiritual striving in his house for the next week.

After a few minutes' silence, Father Theophilos rose from his chair and asked us to join him as he went to the chapel. It was already the Ninth hour and time for Vespers. Time had passed quickly in the kitchen by the long table, around which twenty or so monks could easily squeeze themselves if necessary. The table almost filled the kitchen. The wall between the kitchen and the bedrooms housed a huge stove and oven that served both for cooking and for warming up the bedrooms. Father Theophilos told us that it was used mainly in the winter when the cold wind from the sea found its way into the house through all the cracks in the walls, which were no longer in the best of condition. He used gas for his everyday cooking.

On our way to the chapel Father Theophilos asked me to put my rucksack into my cell next to the kitchen. It was a tiny rectangular room, barely big enough for the bed, a small writing desk and a chair. On the wall there was an icon of the Mother of God, the Theotokos, the celestial patron and protectress of the Holy Mountain. Immediately I felt at home. The cell was like any cell on the Holy Mountain. There were so many familiar things in the midst of the strangeness that everything seemed unreal. Was I on the Holy Mountain or on the monastic island, or was it all just a dream?

Father Theophilos' knocking on my door brought me back to reality. We went through the large living room, which was an annex that had been built later. The *kellion* was originally much smaller, apparently consisting of the kitchen and the wall with the stove that warmed up the three tiny bedrooms behind it. Sofas run against all the walls of the living room, with just one big table in the center. This suggests that there had been many monks living on the island at one time and it might even have been a pilgrimage center, although I cannot see how that would have been possible. In one of the corners there was also a small stove for use on winter days. As we passed through the room, Father Theophilos told us that more than twenty monks had stayed there overnight once when their boat had been washed up into the cave.

We entered the chapel one by one, making the sign of the cross and kissing the icons. I kissed the icon of St. Nicholas with special gratitude. He had protected my voyage and thereby made possible my sojourn on the island of my dreams.

Vespers lasted an hour. Father Theophilos followed the service in the book even though he lived by himself. Christos took up the task of the reader. I was to join in the praying and recitation of "*Kyrie, eleison.*" The atmosphere was cozy and friendly. I thought I could hear in Father Theophilos' voice that he really enjoyed officiating at the service when he had visitors. The chapel was rather dark, despite the oil lamps burning in front of the icons. This is appropriate, as the light symbolizes the divine light that, through Christ, came to the earth darkened by sins. In John (1:9) the coming of Christ is likened to "…the true light which gives light to everyone." Some pericopes later (8:13) we read that Jesus addressed the people: "I am the light of the world. No follower of mine shall walk in darkness; he shall have the light of life." The windows of the chapel were built so that the first rays of the morning sun found their way through them to remind us about the creation of the universe, as related in the book of Genesis. Let us recall the lines: "…The earth was a vast waste, darkness covered the deep, and the spirit of God hovered over the surface of the water. God said, 'Let there be light,' and there was light." The windows did not allow the sun in during the afternoon, and the chapel was much darker then. I liked this order of things. It somehow manifested the mystery of creation and divine light in a way that made the accounts in Genesis and John come alive physically, too.

After Vespers we sat for some time on the balcony at the front of the house, with its small table, three chairs and a bench—all now in the shadow of the day. Most *kellia* have annexed balconies on each side—used in the summer to catch the shade and in the winter for the warmth of the sun. We sat listening to the sounds of the evening as we rested our eyes on the horizon, visible straight in front of us. The sunset turned the sky flaming red like a huge camp fire just before it burns out.

"A beautiful sunset," Christos said, breaking the silence. Father Theophilos held his black rosary between his thumb and forefinger, moving the knots slowly forward one at a time. He was praying silently as he looked out towards the sea. Then Christos reflected aloud that St. Nicholas was the patron saint of sailors, and he recited a modern Greek proverb:

He [St. Nicholas] both assists us on the sea,
And on the land works wondrously.

"*Málista*," Father Theophilos said in approval. "There's also another beautiful poem." He started to recite it:

> Pious sailors once, when sailing,
> Fighting against fierce waves
> With struggles unavailing,
> Shipwrecked nigh through stress of weather,
> Hope of surviving already failing.
> Amid such dangers set,
> Aloud their fate bewailing,
> Lift their voices all together:
>
> "Blessed St. Nicholas, oh, steer us
> From the straits of death so near us
> To the haven of the sea!
> To that harbour in the distance
> Draw us, who dost grant assistance,
> Through the grace of charity!"
>
> Lo! While thus they cried, nor vainly,
> "I am here," a voice said plainly,
> "To watch over you and to aid!"
> Instantly blow favoring breezes,
> Instantly the tempest ceases,
> And to rest the sea is laid.

Father Theophilos lowered his voice as he recited the last line: "And to rest the sea is laid." All three of us remained silent for a while, as after a solemn hymn or the priest's last words at a funeral. Distress is hardly ever greater than when you are out on the merciless sea. It is no wonder that the sailors terrified by the raging storm and the turbulent waves that gradually engulfed their ship shouted for St. Nicholas to rescue them from what seemed to be certain death.

"The distress may be no less on land," Father Theophilos pointed out to us. "The poem shouldn't be taken literally. It's a metaphor, a figure of speech saying: Don't despair. Pray and trust in God!"

How innocent the calm autumn sea appears to be—like a sleeping child, sweet and harmless. What a difference when it wakes up. Its persistent screaming tests the nerves of even the most patient person. The expression "to weather out the storm" is an apt metaphor for coping with the hardships in life. Stretching a point, we could take this to refer to skills similar to surfboarding. We run into many storms in life, with huge dangerous waves that can be surmounted only by surfing through them, using their power and direction to bring us back to safe waters. Going against the waves is foolhardy and can end only in disaster.

To tempt fate is human. In my imagination I find myself with the sailors, and share their fear. I also share their fascination with the powers of the sea. A terrifying voyage is followed by an inexpressible inner peace once a safe haven has been reached. I am convinced that this kind of inner peace can be experienced only after feelings of total helplessness. Perhaps it is the excitement of pushing their luck that makes sailors sail, athletes compete, gamblers gamble. After all, it seems to be the only way of really finding out whether Providence is for or against you. On the other hand, Christ did not throw himself down from the parapet of the temple, because it is written that "you are not to put the Lord your God to the test." This certainly means: don't push your luck! Watch out! In ordinary language, you should not always trust your luck. I was wrapped up in these thoughts, surprised by how expressions from the Gospels were popping up in my mind, when Father Theophilos suddenly brought me back to reality by asking: "Do you have this kind of scenery in Finland?"

"Finland is the land of a thousand lakes," I replied, and then told him about our unique archipelago where I had spent the summers in my youth, fishing and playing the guitar as everyone tended to do in the sixties. Then he asked me all the usual questions, to which I replied: married, three grown-up children, professor at the University of Helsinki, teaching comparative religion, especially monastic life and pilgrimage.

"*Brávo*," he concluded.

"Renéos has also written two books about the Holy Mountain," Christos told him. I was a little surprised that Father Theophilos asked these questions again, as Christos had introduced me to him upon our arrival. Then I thought that perhaps it was his way of making sure that he had got the details right.

"*Brávo*," Father Theophilos repeated. "Now it's time to live the life of spiritual striving."

"Through research we make careers, but by means of spiritual striving we find our roots as human beings," I replied spontaneously.

"To strive is to uproot weeds," Father Theophilos assured us. "We'll start first thing tomorrow."

"I understand that it is a slow and trying task," I said, hesitant.

"It doesn't take long before your eyes see new weeds next to those you have just taken out. The more you uproot them, the more there is to be done."

"Spiritual striving requires much patience and persistent work," Christos pointed out.

"'Keep your mind in hell and despair not,' as my spiritual father used to remind me in my moments of despair," Father Theophilos said. "The reward is immense. You should always keep this in mind when you are facing difficult times."

As soon as the sun had disappeared far out at sea beyond the horizon, the chilly air reached us on the balcony. We went inside to the kitchen for supper. Father Theophilos warmed up the rest of the minestrone soup on the gas cooker, brought out the bread, black olives, tomatoes, and the best wine. He put a huge water jug in the middle of the table. Once he had blessed the food, we all ate rather quickly, hungry as we were, at least Christos and I. Father Theophilos also gave us pieces of halvah, as he thought we needed it to recover our strength. I recalled my summer holidays in the 50s on my grandfather's island in the archipelago, where we were always given halvah in the evening if we had been good during the day. The dry, sweet and filling taste was an echo of my early youth. I really felt at home.

As I was lying in my bed, I could not help thinking how peaceful the day on the island had been, and how well everything had turned out. It all was too good to be true. I knew that I was going to enjoy my stay tremendously, and in the sweetest of contentment I fell sound asleep.

Lessons in Spiritual Striving

I

FATHER THEOPHILOS WOKE ME before sunrise by knocking at my door rhythmically: *ton Adám ton Adám ton amín amín Adám* (Adam, Adam, indeed, indeed, Adam). The rhythm calls us, the descendants of Adam, our forefather, to hurry up to the chapel, the Savior's ark, to take refuge from the Deluge. Although the knocking is an everyday practice in the monasteries on the Holy Mountain, I did not expect Father Theophilos to follow this habit in his solitary *kellion*. On the other hand, when I think about it, it is obvious that a former Athonite will maintain the tradition even if he lives alone when visitors give him the chance to do so. The rhythm of life practiced for decades has become rooted in his heart so that his habits are spontaneous as if they were inherent parts of him.

"I'm already wide awake," I replied. "I'm on my way." The knocking ended as abruptly as it had started and I could hear Father Theophilos' footsteps receding towards the chapel.

I dressed quickly and joined Father Theophilos in the dark chapel. It took some time before I could make him out lighting the oil lamp in front of the icon of St. Nicholas, and also the one above the reader's stand. He moved as gracefully as a shadow and his black *ráson* fluttered like a bat's wings in the dimness. It was only with difficulty that I could see Christos' face as he approached the reader's stand.

Father Theophilos began the morning service by praying in front of the Holy Doors: "Blessed is the Kingdom of the Father, and of the Son, and of the Holy Spirit, now and forever, and to the ages of ages." Christos replied, "Amen" as I did, a little bit behind. Then came the office for the rulers, a reminiscence from the time of the Byzantine Empire. It consists of the two "kingly" Psalms 20 and 21 (*Septuagint,* chapters 19 and 20), and three *troparia* (hymns), in which God and the Mother of God are asked to guard and protect all Orthodox emperors and "the new city (Constantinople), which bears the name of Christ," and to give pious rulers victory over the barbarians. Finally there is a short litany repeating these requests.

This is followed by one of the oldest parts of the office, the main message of which is that God heard man's prayer and sent a Savior to humankind. Christos read the Six Psalms. I found the words of Psalm 142 (*Septuagint* numbering) especially appealing and soothing:

> Lord, hear my prayer;
> listen to my plea;
> in your faithfulness and righteousness answer
>   me.
>
> Do not bring your servant to trial,
> for no person living is innocent before you.
>
> An enemy has hunted me down,
> has crushed me underfoot,
> and left me to lie in darkness like those long
>   dead.
>
> My spirit fails me
> and my heart is numb with despair.
> I call to mind times long past;
> I think over all you have done:
> the wonders of your creation fill my mind
> Athirst for you like thirsty land,
> I lift my outspread hands to you.
>
> Lord, answer me soon;
> my spirit faints.
> Do not hide your face from me

or I shall be like those who go down to the
    abyss.
In the morning let me know of your love,
for I put my trust in you.
Show me the way that I must take,
for my heart is set on you.
Deliver me, Lord, from my enemies;
with you I seek refuge.
Teach me to do your will, for you are my God;
by your gracious spirit guide me on level ground.
Revive me, Lord, for the honour of your name;
be my deliverer; release me from distress.
In your love for me, destroy my enemies
and wipe out all who oppress me,
for I am your servant.

The morning service lasted quite a while. I do not know
exactly how long, because I was lost in the words of the Psalm.
The expression "no person living is innocent before you" brought
to mind what Father Theophilos had said the previous evening:
"The more you practice striving, the more you begin to see your
own faults." With the passing of time, deeds and words reap-
pear in your audio-visual memory, disturbing and distressing
you, bringing about repentance and an intense longing for forgiveness. Spiritual striving implies looking at your life through
a magnifying glass. You see many things you prefer not to see,
and what you think you have forgotten comes back into your
memory requiring resolution. The guilt and repentance you feel
are often so strong that you need the firm support of an experienced spiritual father to guide you to safe waters. Many have
committed suicide as a result of the agony they felt when events
of the past tortured their souls. This is how hard it is to confront
the dark sides of ourselves and how badly we all need forgiveness and the mercy of our Lord. The past cannot be changed, but
with the help of our Lord we may learn to come to terms with
ourselves and our less-than-praiseworthy deeds.

These kinds of experience undoubtedly lie behind David's words. "Lord, hear my prayer," the psalmist pleads in front of his God. "Lord, answer me" he begs piously. "Answer me soon; my spirit faints… or I shall be like those who go down to the abyss. I put my trust in you. Show me the way that I must take… teach me to do your will! …by your gracious spirit guide me… be my deliverer; release me from distress."

It is not difficult to identify oneself with the words of the Psalm. We have all been in situations that we experienced as catastrophes at the time, and it seemed as if there was no way out. Gloomy thoughts filled our minds like dark clouds in the sky and we were in great despair, on the edge of an abyss. But like clouds our thoughts pass away, and it seems like a miracle to feel free again.

It is obvious that the psalmist had experienced this kind of miracle, because in the midst of despair he once again turns to his Lord in prayer asking for his help in his hour of need. He is convinced that, as before, the Lord will now help him across the troubled waters. The sailors also knew this when they cried out for St. Nicholas; the darkest hour is the one before dawn!

We can, as many do, trust only our reason and rational explanation. The comfort this gives in real hours of need is next to none, as we do not have words for what we experience and feel. Therefore, it is no small matter whether we trust in God or not. Those who are used to speaking to God as a friend when their troubles bother them, and also when there are reasons to be thankful, will find the right words to convey what they are going through. The words are not only the words of David, but are common to all humankind. "In the beginning was the Word," John writes, "and what God was, the Word was." To have the Word is to have God!

Hjalmar Sundén regarded the Psalms as pregnant with meaning, because as you read the words you are so easily absorbed in them that you take them as your own. Being able to understand human suffering expressed in words puts our own distress into perspective. The words are, in fact, precise words that break the vicious circle of despair and provide hope for a better future.

My thoughts were running wild about what I understood to be the message in the Psalm when the first rays of the sun suddenly struck the icon of St. Nicholas. The dawn was breaking the darkness, and in an instant I was brought back to reality. Now I had no difficulty seeing the faces of Father Theophilos and Christos. The night was gone, a new day had began.

"Hallelujah!" Christos said loudly as the sunbeams entered the chapel through the window. Then he continued to read the first lines of Psalm 147 (*Septuagint* numbering):

> Praise the Lord!
> Praise the Lord from the heavens;
> praise him in the heights above.
> Praise him, all his angels;
> praise him, all his hosts.
> Praise him, sun and moon;
> praise him, all you shining stars;
> praise him, you highest heavens,
> and you waters above the heavens.
> Let them praise the name of the Lord,
> for by his command they were created;
> he established them for ever and ever
> by an ordinance which will never pass away.

After a brief pause he continued:

> Hallelujah! Praise the Lord from the earth,
> you sea monsters and ocean depths;
> fire and hail, snow and ice,
> gales of wind that obey his voice;
> all mountains and hills;
> all fruit trees and cedars;
> wild animals and all cattle,
> creeping creatures and winged birds.
> Let kings and all commoners,

princes and rulers over the whole earth,
youths and girls,
old and young together,
let them praise the name of the Lord,
for his name is high above all others,
and his majesty above earth and heaven.
He has exalted his people in the pride of power
and crowned with praise his loyal servants.
Praise the Lord.

Christos' reading was impressive. Although I had known him for years, I never imagined him to be so pious. Most of the time he simply fiddles with his machines, dressed in oily jeans and a tee-shirt. It was only from the food he eats that I could have guessed his commitment. He hardly ever eats meat, only lamb at Easter. He always talks about how healthy traditional Greek food is. "Fish clarifies your thoughts," he often tries to convince me. When the first McDonald's restaurants came to the village, he was terrified. "It's the beginning of the end of the world, you know Renéos," he used to tell me almost daily.

From what I heard in the chapel it was apparent that Christos had celebrated the services with Father Theophilos every time he brought him food and stayed overnight. Watching the two men there enjoying every minute of the service, I realized what great performance gifts they both possessed. They were both able to live their parts in the service and turn it into an unforgettable experience. I had never experienced anything even remotely like it before. I would not have been surprised if the Lord himself had been present.

Father Theophilos gave us his blessing at the end of the service, and we then sat for a while on the balcony in the fresh morning air. The sea glittered like a thousand stars from the sun's rays rising over it. There was no land in sight. We had a simple breakfast before Christos departed: the minestrone soup left over from yesterday, bread with honey, black olives, and tomato salad with slices of onions and grapes. Then Father Theophilos made us Greek coffee, which we sipped slowly from the tiny cups.

We accompanied Christos to the lift, which I think could well be regarded as one of the great wonders in this world. The lift itself was the same as any other in old buildings, but the energy that drove it was a new invention. The narrow ravine was a freak of nature, too. It had been eroded over the centuries into a hole at the end of the water-filled cave at the east corner of the cliff. "It's God's gift to us spiritual strivers. It protects us from intruders and pirates," Father Theophilos said as we stood in front of the lift, saying our good-byes and praying for a safe voyage.

When Christos had reached the bottom, Father Theophilos pressed the button to bring the lift up again. Then he told me that the first ascetic living on the island was an exceptionally brave sailor. After his ship had been wrecked in the stormy sea close to the island, he had reached the plateau by climbing up the main mast. When the storm abated he went away, only to return after some time, convinced that it was God's will that he should don the hermit's habit and live on the island. Fishermen brought him food and water and materials to build the monastic cottage. Since then the tradition of spiritual striving has continued unbroken.

2

"Now it's time for our *diakónima*," Father Theophilos said as we entered his house.

"You mean the daily duty?"

"Yes, *diakónima* means a monk's daily duty," he explained.

"What kind of duty do you have in mind?" I asked.

"Obedience is the greatest virtue of them all," he replied. "It drives away arrogance and pride. It's the mother of humility."

"Why is humility so important?" I asked, to check that I had understood him correctly.

"Humility is to submit to the will of our Lord. Adam abandoned the virtue of obedience and therefore fell to the depths of Hades. Christ, on the contrary, was obedient to his Father right to his death on the cross for our salvation. Obedience is our foremost weapon to fight the devil's whispering, which encourages us to show off and take pride in ourselves."

"So humility is the attitude we need if we are to be obedient."

"Yes, and obedience is the forerunner of all virtues. It leads us to the path of virtue and is the only way we can avoid falling into the temptations offered by the devil."

"What's our *diakónima* for today?" I asked a second time.

"Today it's the will of God that we work on the new kitchen garden. This will serve all the hermits our Lord will send here in the future."

Father Theophilos first gave me a black rosary and asked me to put it on my wrist instead of my watch. "You don't need a watch here," he said. Then he took two pairs of gloves from the shelf in the hall and off we went behind the house to continue the work in his kitchen garden that he had begun some time ago.

As we worked arranging the stones, he told me, with an air of satisfaction, that Christos and a friend of his had recently brought a huge amount of fertile soil to the island by helicopter. "The heap is there on your left," he said, pointing out the place to me.

"How often does the helicopter come this way?" I asked.

"It circles this area in search of fires, and at the same time, when it's near enough and there's no emergency, they pop in here for coffee and bring me things for my survival."

"In a way they are obedient, too," I suggested.

"Yes, very much so."

The island badly needed both water and soil. The rocky surface was not ideal for gardening. There was not much earth anywhere, only in the cracks, but then again, when it was raining, water quickly turned these cracks into small basins. Men from Ouranoupolis had worked hard the previous winter cutting stones from the nearby cliff in order to build small terraces for the garden. Most of the stonework had already been done, and it was now our task to arrange the last stones and then to fill the empty rectangles with soil.

As we placed the stones in the terrace-to-be we took turns praying. First Father Theophilos said "Lord Jesus Christ, have mercy on us." I then repeated it and in this way we kept praying unceasingly. The work proceeded slowly. When I tried to hurry it up a bit, Father Theophilos immediately told me that the important thing was not to get the work done quickly, but to pray unceasingly. The work was part of our praying, and praying was the task. The terrace was only the by-product.

Despite the prayer, my thoughts went astray time and again. I looked at Father Theophilos in his black *ráson* with his tanned face. He was sweating quite heavily as the sun rose higher, and it became warmer as the house sheltered us from the wind. I wondered how he could manage without dropping to the ground with fatigue in his thick black clothes. I felt a little dizzy in the sun, so I covered my head with an old white hat I had in my pocket. I needed to protect my developing baldness from sunburn. Father Theophilos smiled when he looked at my hat, but did not comment on it in any way. He simply continued to pray in a low voice: "Lord Jesus Christ, have mercy on us." So did I, following his example, and our work proceeded with the labor of both our hands and prayer.

Father Theophilos was a little shorter than me, perhaps one meter and sixty-five centimeters. His thin but tough disposition reflected inner calmness and wisdom. His appearance was that of determination and his clear blue eyes looked innocent against his nicely tanned face. From his long grey beard one could easily have mistaken him for someone quite old, as his long hair tied in a knot behind his head was completely grey. I knew that the Greeks' hair greys quite early and therefore concluded that he was still less than 60 years old. My estimation proved to be correct. Later he told me that he had recently reached the age of fifty-seven.

Father Theophilos' features were so slender and atypical in Greece that I suspected him of being of noble birth. To make sure, I asked him,

"*Géronda*, where in Greece do you come from?"

"From Athens," he replied, somewhat embarrassed. My question had interrupted our prayer.

"You're Christos' cousin?"

"My father was the elder brother of Christos' father. My mother comes from an old noble family in Athens. Here I am only an old hermit, working on my inner life. These worldly things are of no significance."

"Lord Jesus Christ, have mercy on me." I was anxious to point out that it was not my intention to interrupt our praying. Father Theophilos smiled. We prayed for another three hours until the sun was almost at its zenith. It was so hot that working became unbearable. Although Father Theophilos had emphasized that the main motive was not to get the terrace done as quickly as possible, but to show persistence in obedience, we continued to labor until it became impossible to go on.

"Building a simple terrace in the burning sun bends our own will to follow the will of God," he remarked, as he paused for a minute.

Persistence in habit is inevitable, because our nature always tends to look for the easiest and shortest way to the goal. The goal, however, is to build the path, and its length depends on how willing we are to give up our conveniences and our own will to fulfil God's will. Humans are by nature obstinate. Therefore the path is long and difficult.

"Enough striving for the moment," Father Theophilos suddenly announced, to my great relief. "Let's go to the *kellion* and rest for a while. You're not used to manual labor in the heat the way I am."

He was quite right. I was already exhausted. I am sure I would not have lasted much longer. When we entered the house I went straight into the bathroom. I felt dizzy so I washed my face with cold water. What a relief—paradise! When I went back to the kitchen I realized how tired I really was. I drank many glasses of water. Father Theophilos noticed my state and gave me a little *raki* and some pieces of sweet Turkish delight. We rested for half an hour in the kitchen, sipping our drinks and talking.

"It's not easy to follow the will of God," he said. "It requires a lot of work physically, but above all spiritually." He was apparently pleased with my commitment so far.

"It's hard work all right," I replied. I was so tired that it was obvious that I could not help but agree with him.

"Let me tell you an anecdote," he continued. "An archer was practising in a forest near St. Antony's cave when he heard hearty laughter from the group of hermits standing around the ascetic. Eventually the loud noise started to irritate the archer as it disturbed his concentration. Their cheerfulness made him envious. He hurried angrily to the holy fathers and reproached them for being insincere: 'Why are you laughing? You should be working!' St. Antony asked him calmly to lend him his bow and arrow so that he could show him what it was all about. When he held it in his hands he began slowly to pull the string more and more until the archer suddenly shouted: 'Don't pull it any more. You'll break it!' St. Antony loosened the string and gave back the bow and arrow, saying: 'Spiritual striving also has its limits!'"

"This morning surely taught me that lesson," I assured the hermit.

"Now it's time to pray and rest," he said. "You may go to your room now. I'll wake you up in time for vespers. There are some books on the shelves in the living room, the *Philokalia* for example, in case you want something to read in your cell."

"Thank you."

"There's also a translation of it in English. The translator stayed here some years ago in order to understand the spirit of spiritual striving."

"I'll find the books."

"Take some water and fruit from the kitchen if you feel tired," he added before he went into his cell to pray.

Father Theophilos kept to his schedule despite my presence in his *kellion*. This was, of course, to be expected. Why should he change his daily routine because of my short visit? He carried out his duties as he had done for most of his adult life, an Athonite habit whose present rhythm was established more than a thousand years ago. I felt honoured to be able to stay in the house of this very special hermit, especially because I knew that he seldom received guests. It was not that he did not like people, he merely wanted to spend his whole life in obedience to the will of God. If it were God's will for someone to visit him, then he happily accepted that. Realizing this, I felt blessed.

I followed Father Theophilos' advice and went into the living room to get the first volume of the *Philokalia*, the collection of texts written between the fourth and fifteenth centuries by spiritual virtuosos of the Orthodox Christian tradition. It is a collection of sayings in which the holy fathers discuss how the intellect is to be purified, illumined and made perfect. *Philokalia* means "love of the beautiful," and it is understood as the transcendent source of life and the revelation of Truth. From the text we learn how to awaken and develop attention and consciousness. We learn how to attain that state of watchfulness that is the hallmark of sanctity. The *Philokalia* is an itinerary revealing a spiritual path and inducing us to follow it. It teaches us to overcome ignorance, to uncover the knowledge that lies within, to rid ourselves of illusion, and to be receptive to the grace of the Holy Spirit, which shows all things and brings all things to remembrance.

I read all this in the introduction to the first volume. Recalling Father Theophilos' anecdote about St. Antony I immediately looked up what the "first" hermit had to teach us about the character of man and about a virtuous life:

> Men are often called intelligent wrongly. Intelligent men are not those who are erudite in the sayings and books of the wise men of old, but those who have an intelligent soul and can discriminate between good and evil. They avoid what is sinful and harms the soul; and with deep gratitude to God they resolutely adhere by dint of practice to what is good and benefits the soul. These men alone should truly be called intelligent.

I read the passage three times, as is customary in the liturgy. Then, exhausted by the toils of the morning, I lay down on my bed and instantly fell sound asleep.

3

Once again I woke up to the rhythmic knocking at my door: *ton Adám ton Adám ton amín amín Adám.* It was time for vespers. Father Theophilos roused me from my afternoon nap as he had done early in the morning. It was all so familiar to me from my fieldwork on the Holy Mountain. I had no watch, but from the sun I knew that it was already past four o'clock. There was no need for a watch here, because the hermit applied the Athonite rhythm as far as possible. It was my duty to submit to his schedule, leave everything to him and simply act on command.

Father Theophilos asked me to be the reader in the absence of Christos. I felt honored, but at the same time afraid I would not be up to the task. I had never been a church reader before, much less in Greek. Nor did I expect this kind of total commitment. However, there was not much time to ponder about it, and I started slowly to read the psalm praising the Lord as the creator of everything.

> Bless the Lord, my soul.
> Lord my God, you are very great,
> clothed in majesty and splendor,
> and enfolded in a robe of light.
> You have spread out the heavens like a tent,
> and laid the beams of your dwelling on the
>   waters;
> you take the clouds for your chariot,
> riding on the wings of the wind;
> you make the winds your messengers,
> flames of fire your servants;
> you fixed the earth on its foundation
> so that it will never be moved.

The deep covered it like a cloak,
and the waters stood above the mountains.
At your rebuke they fled,
at the sound of your thunder they rushed away,
flowing over the hills,
pouring down into the valleys
to the place appointed for them.
You fixed a boundary which they were not to
    pass;
they were never to cover the earth again…
All of them look to you in hope
to give them their food when it is due.
What you give them they gather up;
when you open your hand, they eat their fill of
    good things.
When you hide your face, they are dismayed.
When you take away their spirit, they die
and return to the dust from which they came.
When you send forth your spirit, they are
    created,
and you give new life to the earth.
May the glory of the Lord stand for ever,
and may the Lord rejoice in his works!
When he looks at the earth, it quakes;
when he touches the mountains, they pour forth
    smoke.
As long as I live I shall sing to the Lord;
I shall sing psalms to my God all my life long.
May my meditation be acceptable to him;
I shall delight in the Lord.
May sinners be banished from the earth
and may the wicked be no more!
Bless the Lord, my soul.
Praise the Lord.

While I was reading, I was constantly aware that my pro-nunciation was not entirely correct. Father Theophilos seemed pleased that I made the effort, however. After the litanies he then asked me to read Psalms 140, 141, 129 and 116 (*Septuagint* numbering). At the end of the service he blessed me. I felt a warmth in my heart. After the service we again moved to the balcony to have our tea and cake. We sat for quite some time in silence, drinking our tea and gazing at the display of colors on the horizon.

"Renéos, tell me about your dream," Father Theophilos suddenly asked me.

I told him the whole story of my odyssey in the library, the lithograph of Coronelli and my dream about the hermit living on the monastic island. He was surprised, or so I gathered from the sudden rise of his grey eyebrows. "It certainly was God's will that you should come here," he said.

"How do you know that it is a thought or vision inspired by God and not a fantasy or suggestion coming from the devil?" I asked him, in the hope of gaining a more profound understanding of these elusive spiritual matters.

"For a long time now you have been living a life in suspense. Your heart has become open to things divine and ready to listen to the will of God," he explained. "When you really make an effort to find a resolution to things that trouble you, it announces itself."

"Was the dream my resolution?"

"Yes."

"But the dream was only a picture of a place. I'm perplexed. Now that I'm here I don't know what I should do or ask."

"Maybe you're not meant to ask anything, only to experience."

"Are you sure that my dream was not merely the product of my wishful thinking? I'm so drained and frustrated by the bureaucracy at the university, the endless e-mails and administrative paperwork that are increasing totally out of proportion to what we as professors really should be doing, which is research and teaching."

"Your dissatisfaction with the way things are now at your university may have triggered your need to search for a solution to the anguish you have experienced, but that's not the whole truth."

"I simply cannot become a robot shifting papers from one pile to another, incoming and outgoing, writing reports and letters of introduction, recommendations, references and so forth day after day in an ever-increasing amount. The argumentative atmosphere at the meetings drains my energy and distracts me so much that I find it difficult to collect myself and concentrate on my research and teaching, which after all is what I should be doing in the first place. Creativity dries up and this is the most disturbing part. Time seems to be running out. It is as if I were being buried alive. There is no point in living when there is no flow of thought, no inspiration, no enthusiasm, no reward, all of which creativity gives me when things seem to go my way."

"You've tasted the sweetness of the flow of thought. I can see that losing that divine feeling makes you miserable." Father Theophilos comforted me.

"Yes, I hate being at a standstill."

"Dear Renéos, we are all created in the image of God. This means that inherent in us is the divine energy of God. It's not the essence, but the energy of God. This energy is present in all creativity. Whenever we create anything the energy of God is reflected in that creation."

"That explains it!" I was ecstatic. "You're quite right. That is why it's so therapeutic and so rewarding to allow your inherent energy to flow into art and scholarly work. This is why, with all my heart, I want to fulfil my potential. I need to make my project come true."

"Dear Renéos, you should not see it so much as your project. It should rather be regarded as making the will of God come true."

"But there are so many things that I'd like to understand and there's far too little time to accomplish what I want to accomplish."

"You're quite right in that, but sometimes the bureaucratic nonsense can also be trials put in front of you by God so that you can see his will more clearly," Father Theophilos explained. "Creativity also dries up if you are in a constant state of bliss, because being creative requires some tension that forces your thoughts into movement."

"I've certainly been living in the midst of tensions. There's no denying that," I said with a hint of irony.

Father Theophilos listened attentively to my outburst. Then we sat quietly together while I continued to reflect upon my situation. "It seems as if there is something inside me that now requires more attention."

"This is what trials are for," he explained. "When there's trouble there's also a resolution. The task is simply to find it."

"I've tasted the sweetness of creativity. That's why administration is so dull to me. The more I listen to my inner voice, the more attention it demands."

"This is how it is. It's a matter of priority. Have you followed the suggestions of the time-waster demon whispering, 'First you have to finish this task before you can feel free to do what you really want to do'?"

"Well put. How did you know I'm one of his victims?"

"The desert fathers long ago identified the demon's ways of leading us astray from the path put before us by our Lord."

Feeling a bit ashamed of myself for having poured out my troubles to Father Theophilos, I tried to excuse myself by saying that I was very grateful to him for his hospitality, and that I knew how difficult it must have been to put up all the pilgrims and visitors on the Holy Mountain. "The Athonites are in an awkward situation, too. The pilgrims take up time the monks would like to use for prayer."

"Serving the pilgrims is also a *diakónima*," Father Theophilos replied. "It's through serving others that one fulfils the will of God."

"Isn't it difficult to make progress on the spiritual path in the midst of all the visitors?"

"It can sometimes be trying," he confessed. "There are fewer visitors during the winter, so there's plenty of time for prayer then."

"But you left the Holy Mountain to live here as a hermit?"

"It was the will of God for me to devote all my time to him."

"The situation is very similar in the arts, in scholarly work and science. Creative minds want to devote all their time to their work. This is what makes the conflict of interests at the university so difficult. Those in the administration don't always understand that they should have patience and let us work in peace. The results will eventually turn up, but we need time."

I felt quite comfortable talking to Father Theophilos. Everything just came out of me and there was no way I could have stopped my outburst.

"Statistically I have about ten more creative years. If it's God's will, I may have even more. Then I'd be a lucky man. But I may equally well have only a few years left."

"This is the reality of life."

"This is why every day has become important to me. I no longer want to do things that distract and hinder me from bringing my inner life into blossom."

Father Theophilos listened to me and then raised his index finger by way of emphasis. "We should above all submit to the will of God. It's essential that you realize what duty our Lord has assigned to you. You must carefully study whether your goal is God's will or not."

"How do I know what the will of God is?" I asked anxiously.

"When creative water from the inner well begins to flow naturally and you're perplexed by the beauty it produces, you are on the right path," he replied.

"Being in touch with the creativity in oneself is not easy in the midst of societal duties. When I was writing my Master's thesis, my research totally absorbed me. Having completed my studies, I was offered a research fellowship. I really enjoyed working in the library and conducting field research. I did research for years, only to end up as a senior lecturer when the fellowship expired."

"Don't you like teaching?"

"I do enjoy teaching, but there's no time for research. That's the problem. There's a conflict of interest. I'm constantly longing for research time."

"But you have time between terms, don't you?"

"The summer is short in Finland. The term ends in May, but I have administrative duties during the first weeks in June. Then, after the long winter, I don't have the energy to carry out effective research. July is supposed to be the summer holiday month. The first half of August is a good time to study, but then in the middle of the month, duty calls me to planning meetings for the Michelmas term that begins in early September. The time for research is, in practice, next to nothing."

"You trained yourself to do research, but ended up as a teacher. Is that what you're saying?"

"Yes. I was naive. I thought that being a professor meant doing research more or less full time, with some teaching in between. I was so wrong. Administration takes up most of my time, then teaching, and finally, if I still have energy, there is research. Today, creativity is possible only during my sabbaticals. It's depressing to realize that I have to postpone my enthusiasm for study until I retire."

"You need a job, of course," Father Theophilos remarked. "But that is a compromise not always to one's taste."

"The university requires more of us each year. The pace is getting tougher and there is constant pressure to be accountable. Colleagues in their early fifties are burned out. Those who are conscientious too often end up dead prematurely."

"The situation is much the same here in Greece," Father Theophilos replied. "Now and again I get letters from pilgrims asking for advice on precisely these matters. You're right that it's not unimportant what kind of attitude you have towards the demon exploiter of your time, especially in mid-life."

"My life is running out like the sand in an hourglass. Some people are still creative after retirement, but you cannot count on that. Many think that when they retire they will be able to do all those things they had no time for during their working life. Although one may have many years to go, old age is usually overshadowed by illness. Only a few people manage to carry out their postponed plans."

"I wouldn't advise anyone to leave things undone that can be done today. If our Lord calls us today, then today is the day we should submit to that calling."

"But the callings are often so diffuse."

"It's true. It's not easy to distinguish between calling and deception."

"First I felt a calling to study theology, then comparative religion and especially Buddhism. Studying is creative activity, but in scholarly work the creativity is confined to scientific discourse. Artistic discourse is more free and experimental. It allows us to transform our inner visions into art and put them on display. It's not the final word. Each piece of art is only a step in an unknown direction. For years I have felt a conflict between the artistic and the scholarly me."

"As humans we're not only cognitive but also affective beings. Therefore we have to cultivate a balance between our emotional and logical thinking. It's not good to split them up too much."

I told Father Theophilos about Max Müller's (d. 1900) resolve. He has been regarded as one of the founders of comparative religion. As a man of philology he was strict in his scholarly work, but nevertheless felt a deep sympathy with Indian religious thought, both Hindu and Buddhist. While translating their sacred texts, he also kept a diary in which he jotted down his personal thoughts and feelings about religion and life in general. This has also been my resolve. My fieldwork diaries contain notes of what I have studied, and also more personal observations. Like Müller, I have been keeping a distance from my artistic self. Until very recently I have been quite content with this arrangement. However, now the inner tension has become unbearable. The artist in me no longer wants to play second fiddle. "He insists on becoming the first violin."

"You cannot suppress the flow of creativity," Father Theophilos warned me. "Before too long it will force itself through like a volcanic eruption and that can be very harmful to your mental health."

"I know. I've deliberately chosen the easy and safe way, and poured water on my smoldering artistic fire. Now I've reached the day of reckoning."

Father Theophilos listened carefully to my outpourings and then he said: "It's imperative that you reconcile the artist and the scholar in you. What do you mean by 'the artist in me'?"

"It's the peace in creativity."

"Can you explain that to me, too?"

"Creativity has a rhythm and tone of its own. It implies listening peacefully to the integrating harmonies, enjoying them and understanding their message."

"Aren't there also disharmonies in creativity?"

"Of course. Creativity oscillates between harmonies and disharmonies, alternating like waves in the sea. When I'm totally absorbed in creativity, I experience glimpses of insights into the conditions of life, into being in this world and into life after death. These are moments of bliss. There's no fear. I can sincerely say that I feel completely at ease at that moment."

Father Theophilos was silent for a while, and then said: "You did the right thing in coming here. It's important to distance oneself from conflicts and troubles from time to time. In everyday life it's sometimes impossible to see clearly which path to take at the crossroads."

"I really feel I'm at a crossroads in my life."

"Years ago I was in a similar situation," the hermit confessed. "I was studying at Oxford. My parents were well-off and my mother's family lived there. First I enjoyed the terms tremendously. The lectures and the parties, or rather the parties and some lectures, were great fun. Then the gap between book learning and the richness of my inner life started to bother me. I didn't want to waste my time partying, and the knowledge in the books seemed too bleak compared to what I'd expected."

"How did you manage to break the bonds of family ties and expectations?"

"I'd visited the Holy Mountain a few times. There I met an old *géronda*, a very spiritual monk. His clear thoughts impressed me so much that I decided right on the spot to become a monk. For years he was my beloved spiritual father." When Father Theophilos said "beloved," his voice became emotional and his eyes moistened.

"Don't you ever miss company?"

"Ten times a year I take part in the services on the Holy Mountain, usually the all-night vigils, *agrypnía*. Christos brings me food once a week. Occasionally he brings a friend with him. Spiritual striving is tough. It requires concentration and quietness, which is hard to find in the midst of people."

"How true," I remarked. "Artists and scientists also withdraw to peaceful settings to be focused and creative. Even ordinary people often prefer country living, deliberately avoiding the noise and temptations of the cities."

Father Theophilos did not comment, so I continued: "The life of a scholar resembles spiritual striving. It's a kind of desert life, too. The scholar is a lonely one who struggles to solves problems, aiming to understand and to explain. Not everyone realizes that research requires a rhythm of its own. That pace conflicts with the expectations of everyday life. Not everyone understands what it implies to be a scholar living in the midst of societal duties.

"Many of my friends from Oxford, who ended up as professors, have had the same complaints," Father Theophilos said. "In mid-life they had difficulties balancing their duties and their inner calling. In their letters they have told me about these tensions and have asked me for advice. Some, like myself, have even left their chair at the university, which came as a surprise to their colleagues."

"This also happens in Finland. At one time many professors were leaving to edit daily newspapers or weekly religious magazines," I said. "The words in the *Psalms*, 'In the path that I should take they have hidden a snare for me' are equally true for spiritual and academic strivers. Both have to avoid falling into the temptations and trends of our time. What is fashionable today may seem gratifying at first. Swimming with the tide will, however, prove to be regrettable in the end. Both have to struggle hard to stay on the narrow path."

"You shouldn't give even an inch to the Tempter," Father Theophilos warned me. "There's no playing around with the devil, who can appear in a thousand shapes. It's almost impossible to detect the tricks of transformation unless you're on your guard all the time."

"How do you recognize the tricks of the Deceiver?"

"If I knew the answer to that, I wouldn't have to live the life of an ascetic. There is one piece of advice I can give you. Whenever you have second thoughts about anything, you should follow that instinct and opt out of any agreement. A vigilant mind usually warns us by means of second thoughts, doubts and a sense of discontent when we have made an error of judgement. Follow that lead!"

"I'm at that crossroads, aren't I?"

"So it seems. Now it's time for supper. Even spiritual striving has its limits, as St. Antony taught us."

4

FATHER THEOPHILOS FILLED THE kitchen table with small plates of appetizers, as is the custom in Greek *tavernas*: Greek salad, small fried sardine-like fish, black olives, cheese, pieces of hard dry bread softened in a saucepan of water. There was also a carafe of water and another of red wine.

"The desert," he explained, "is the home of the devil. For centuries the desert fathers have been bravely fighting the battle against an invisible and devious enemy regarded as a painter, a serpent of many forms feeding on the fires of passion, a breeder of fantasies par excellence. These Christian soldiers have held their positions to the bitter end, but with the help and mercy of our Lord, they have won the greatest victory of all—eternal life."

"Isn't the desert also the garden in which spiritual life is brought under cultivation?" I wanted to check my understanding.

"Yes, the desert is the Garden of our Lord. His eyes are watching every step of the sincere spiritual striver. He will save the soul of the warrior in his hour of need. The desert is therefore an fitting place for spiritual heroism."

"I've read that this desert is a very dangerous place for those who have no proper education or guidance in spiritual matters."

"I wouldn't advise anyone to don the habit of a spiritual striver without the guidance of a spiritual father."

"To read about the Tempter in Matthew is of course not the same as meeting him in person in the desert. It must be a terrifying experience."

"It is terrifying, but as our Lord says, we're not to live by bread alone, but by every word that comes from the mouth of God."

"I've read that monks drive away the Tempter by reciting the Jesus prayer. Am I right?"

"Yes, reciting 'Lord Jesus Christ, have mercy on me' is the best way of fighting the demons in their various manifestations."

"Do you think this would also work for the scholar struggling with the demons of doubt in the desert of his or her study, or in the library?"

"Of course, if you submit to the will of our Lord, He will show you the narrow path between hell and despair."

"It was a long time before I found my own rhythm and the meaningfulness in enduring the loneliness inherent in scholarly work, and before I managed to convince myself that there was light at the end of the tunnel. Doubt and despair were daily companions when I was working on my doctoral thesis."

"You're quite right in identifying the whisperer as the Tempter," Father Theophilos assured me. "Doubts are often the whispers of the Tempter. You just have to remember that there's a difference between doubts and second thoughts."

"What kind of difference?"

"For example, when you're asked to write an entry in an encyclopedia, your immediate response is that you're honoured and that you'd like to do it. Then, suddenly you hear the warning bells of doubt that you're not really up to it and that therefore you should drop it. In this case it is better for you to put your faith in God and trust that you will find a way of doing it in the end. The impossible becomes possible by taking one step at a time. Eventually the task will be done."

"What about those second thoughts?"

"Second thoughts are more like intuition, energies from God trying to put you on the right track, as it were. In any case, you must listen carefully to your thoughts, express them aloud, then listen to them again and consider them, then finally, with discernment, make your judgement. Practice makes perfect. But you should start now, not wait until tomorrow!"

"So by identifying the Tempter or the tricks played or fantasies painted by him, I can resist falling into the traps along the narrow path to spiritual integrity?"

"You're as good a scholar as you'd like to be, but you need to dispel your doubts about your own abilities. The life of a scholar truly resembles that of an ascetic striver."

"Indeed it does. Many scholars are exhausted by their basic research and slow progress. At one point or another they fall into despair, convinced that it is all a waste of time. Research requires humility, which is not much favoured in our society today. The competition for a chair begins as soon as you have published one monograph and some articles. The *streber* is born and what is worse, the *streber* usually gets the chair. All too many sacrifice almost everything to become a professor, neglect their family, devote a lot of time to intrigue, and are drained of their humanity in pursuit of their goal."

"Is it really worth it?" Father Theophilos asked.

"It means everything to some scholars. A friend of mine told me that she had sacrificed everything for her chair, her husband and family. When she became professor she was happy but perplexed: 'Is this what I have paid so dearly for?' she asked herself. You see, there are so few chairs and tenured positions at the university nowadays. Most jobs are part-time or fixed-term."

"So young scholars feel insecure and unprovided for."

"Yes. The joy of having a chair is very short-lived compared to the drudgery of the ant-like life that follows, fighting with colleagues, engaging in power-plays and drowning in innumerable administrative duties. Many end up defending their school of thought and their department, and applying for funds like a beggar."

"There's not much fun in that," Father Theophilos said with a smile.

"Almost all my friends are divorced, some more than once. Many suffer from stress-related illnesses and loss of perspective. They grow old prematurely."

"The autumn of life should be the most beautiful and pleasant phase," Father Theophilos said with an air of contentment. "Especially when aging follows its natural course. I've always admired the lively eyes of old monks, their childish curiosity and mature wisdom. Don't you find this in the eyes of old professors?"

"Sometimes—in the eyes of those who have managed to avoid getting involved in all the politics. There's a very good poem by the Swedish poet Alf Henriksson. I'll translate it for you:

WHILE ACADEMICS QUARREL

This I will tell you as an elderly Confessor:
Dear son, never become an Oxford Professor!
And if you're thinking to cast your net wider,
Do not aspire to Cambridge either!

I have met four, I have met five.
No expression of joy in their faces survive.
By the tree of knowledge there is no mother,
Only a circle of academics who hate each other.

I urge you, therefore, as an elderly Confessor:
My dear, never become an Oxford Professor!
For your happiness and peace of mind I add the
    rider,
Do not aspire to Cambridge either!

"Society has certainly changed rapidly in recent years," Father Theophilos reflected. "The baby-boom generation is a victim of war, too, I suppose. The need to rebuild society triggered tough piecework agreements and the ideology that work ennobles man."

"Work is the God of our time, and especially the money that goes with it."

"Perhaps it's really the individualistic idea that money gives freedom, for women the freedom to choose whether to stay in a marriage or not, for men a feeling of authority and power in society."

"Freedom is an illusion. Those addicted to work grow old quickly. Values in life become distorted. To regard other people as instruments, as a means to an end, as robots, is fatal to yourself. Death therefore comes suddenly, unexpectedly."

"Many a pilgrim complained to me about these things during my time on the Holy Mountain," Father Theophilos told me.

"Being aware of this," I continued, "I need to resolve the conflict in me between my sense of duty and the voice of my inner calling."

"You need to map out all the factors involved, and put them in order and perspective. Then you will see some results from your striving."

"My dilemma is that, although it is prestigious and financially secure to pursue an academic career, being a professor hinders creativity. Do I have the courage to submit to my inner calling? It involves tramping along uncleared paths. It's hard work following the voice. I very much doubt my ability to do it."

"Don't forget that the compass of enquiry should be God's will," Father Theophilos reminded me. "When you follow God's will, you cannot fail. Pray for that advice. You've found the path. Don't go astray. Be observant and proceed slowly so that you don't lose sight of it."

"Easier said than done," I complained. "Here, on the island, in your *kellion*, everything seems clear. In everyday life, in the midst of my activities and duties, I lose sight of the path, the awareness is elsewhere, and things get out of hand."

"Keep a diary," Father Theophilos suggested. "Record every day on paper! After a week, a month, a year, when you reread what you have jotted down, you will rediscover your thoughts and resolutions and find the fork where you went off in the wrong direction. With your diary as your compass you will keep on the right track. Because the delay is short, going astray for a little while won't cause too much damage in the long run."

After the meal Father Theophilos quickly put all the remaining food into the fridge. I helped him wash the dishes. Then we went onto the balcony. The sun was about to set for the day. It was a habit of the hermit's to rest his eyes and mind by watching the spectacle of the horizon, the images of our Lord's energies, as he understood the colorful display at sunset.

This evening the multicolored horizon was, once again, spellbinding. It was already so late that, to our disappointment, it was not long before the full moon appeared in the sky, reflecting a silvery bridge across the sea straight in front of us all the way to our island. It was as if the energies of our Lord were softly touching us, encouraging us to proceed with our enterprise. The view was carved permanently into my mind.

"Wherever man is, the moon created by our Lord greets everyone as He shows mercy to everyone who seeks refuge in Him," Father Theophilos said. Was he reading my thoughts?

After sunset we went to the chapel. Father Theophilos kissed the icon of St. Nicholas to show his respect for its miracles. Then he recited the Jesus Prayer, raising and lowering his voice like the waves in the sea, "Lord Jesus Christ, have mercy on us." I followed his rhythm as he recited the words, whispering until he gradually allowed his voice to fade away into the silence of the night.

Before I fell asleep I listened for quite some time to the lapping of the waves, the eternal breathing of the sea and the wind reaching the rocky shore, as all monks must have done at night since the first hermit arrived on the island. I felt part of that lineage. I was happy that, despite my doubts, I had ventured on this journey. Most of all, I was pleased with myself that I had followed my inner calling and reassumed the direction of my life.

5

Mᴇʏ sᴏᴊᴏᴜʀɴ ᴏɴ ᴛʜᴇ ᴍᴏɴᴀsᴛɪᴄ island passed all too quickly. The daily routines consisted of eight hours of offices and prayer, eight hours of work and eight hours of rest, not pursued in succession, but intermingled. The hours of rest were, in fact, laborious. To confess and discuss your innermost feelings and thoughts is not idleness, but painstaking and exhausting. The nights were short due to the early offices and the intensity of the evening discussions, which kept my thoughts whirling around in my head into the small hours. Only with great difficulty and with persistent recitation of the Jesus Prayer did I finally fall asleep.

The evening and morning services followed the daily cycle of offices and hours of prayer in the Byzantine rite, rooted in the first five centuries A.D. During the decades of persecution the Christians had to hold their offices of communal worship in the evening, at midnight, and in the early morning. When the persecution stopped, they also held them during the day, following the Roman system. The twenty-four hours of the day were divided into eight periods of three hours each. The counting of the hours began at sunrise and sunset, which meant that the calculation followed the cycle of the sun. The four canonical "hours" of the day were thus fixed: 6 A.M. (First), 9 A.M. (Third), 12 noon (Sixth) and 3 P.M. (Ninth).

The monks on the Holy Mountain of Athos have preserved this Byzantine rite so that their daily schedule differs from that of the world with regard to time and the experience of time. First, they still use the Julian calendar, which is thirteen days behind the Gregorian one that is in use elsewhere. Were I to step off the ferry at Daphne on September 9th, as I have done for many years, it would be August 28th when I stood on the jetty. Second, the periods of daylight and darkness are each divided into twelve equal parts, each part consisting of one hour. At sunrise and sunset it is twelve o'clock, and one hour later it is one o'clock. The new day, or the next twenty-four-hour period, begins at sunset. Sunrise and sunset are defined as the moments when the first or last rays of the sun strike the summit of Mount Athos. Therefore the time alters as the seasons change. In most of the monasteries the clocks point to twelve at sunset, when it is no more than eight o'clock Greek time, and thus the time on the Holy Mountain is about four hours ahead. Monastic life, then, follows the rhythm of nature. As a former Athonite, Father Theophilos started his day at sunset, which also explained why the moments on the balcony were so significant. He celebrated Vespers about an hour and a half before sunset, which was a time for reflection upon the beauty of our Lord's creation. "Sunset is my TV," he used to say. "At sunset I see and hear the energies of our Lord."

Father Theophilos asked me to assist him as a reader at both the evening and morning services. My Greek was not very good, but my slowness did not seem to bother him at all, rather the contrary. It gave him even more time to listen to the words of our Lord. It became my duty to read the Psalms and the extracts from the Gospel. After my first service he told me that by reading I would be an integral part of the liturgical order of life and time on the island, and would more quickly learn to understand the Orthodox view of life. I found this highly rewarding, because one of the aims in my studies on monasteries and pilgrimage had, in fact, been to find out what my life would be like if I were living the life of a monk. However, I also suspected that Father Theophilos enjoyed listening to the voice of another human being after all his lonely days on the island, thus experiencing a liturgy rather than the prayer of a hermit.

The kitchen-garden terrace proceeded quickly and on our third day it was completed. The weather became much cooler, and that made all the difference to our work. Despite the fact that Father Theophilos pointed out to me several times that getting the work done quickly was not as significant as proceeding in prayer, he was clearly satisfied when the terrace was ready. We filled it with fertile soil and planted onions.

It had rained for two nights in a row and all the reservoirs were full of refreshing water. Father Theophilos said to me that our Lord had seen our work and listened to our prayer, and had now given us water. "Lord Jesus Christ, have mercy on us," he said, making the sign of the cross as he did so.

The evenings on the balcony were when we had time for discussion. When the sun had set, the moon rose. Every evening its silvery bridge called us into the landscape of our subconscious. Gradually the worries of everyday life at home fell into oblivion. The experiences of the present overwhelmed me. My inner life seemed more real than my outer circumstances. My mind became totally absorbed in listening to the will of God.

"The view from the balcony is like paradise, isn't it?" Father Theophilos said many times, but then he warned me, "It's all eyewash. When the calm sea begins to rage and the gales are blowing, a sailor's life is sheer hell. Likewise, a hermit's life is peaceful at times, but even an experienced ascetic is overcome by hellish tribulations now and again."

"Isn't it more difficult to be a monk when you're young?"

"It is, but you can never lay yourself to rest before you're in your grave. The Tempter is so devious and reckless. In the garden I have to uproot weeds every day, and the more I pull up, the more there are underneath. It's a never-ending story. With every weed of my inner life I see more weeds, and therefore the older you get the more you see. Only the mercy of our Lord can save us from despair."

During the pauses in our discussions we listened silently to the evening concert of the cicadas. The breeze and the chirping were like a duet, one louder than the other. As the wind stopped, the cicadas became cheerful, and when the breeze came up, they fell silent for a while. I was already in deep meditation, lulled by the sounds of nature and the silence, when Father Theophilos began to think aloud.

"Each of us is an unknown pilgrim," he said. "The pilgrimage lasts a lifetime. The further we travel into the landscape of our inner world, the more we learn to know the unknown pilgrim in us. Don't ask: 'Who am I?' Ask: 'Into what kind of flower am I to blossom?'"

"Do you mean that there's a unique task reserved for each of us?"

"Yes. Everyone has a special talent," he assured me. "The meaning of life is to see it blossom. This is God's will, because your talent is of the image of God. We should live in accordance with that image."

"*Géronda*," I confessed, "in the evening, when I'm lying in my bed, before falling asleep, pictures and thoughts rise from deep inside to the surface of my mind, compelling me to examine myself. Some of my vices are displayed so openly that it's easy to recognize and register them. Others are more hidden and lurk in the corner. These are more devious, but still, over the years I have learned to deal with them, too. Then there are vices that are not always present but recur at intervals. These are the most trouble-some. Like squabbling enemies they spring upon me when the opportunity presents itself, and allow me to be neither prepared as in war nor off guard as in peace."

"This certainly sounds like the Tempter," Father Theophilos concluded. "Can you give me an example?"

"Well, I'm emotional, even romantic deep inside. However, in everyday life I have to be rational. I can live up to that stan-dard for quite a while, but then to my own surprise, time and time again, I fall into bad ways, drink too much, hang around in the bars and pubs, end up in bad company, only to wake up with a terrible hangover and pangs of remorse. When I'm in that state, I resolve never to drink again, as I know that one thing will lead to another and it has proved impossible to resist the whis-pers of the devil."

"It certainly is the devious devil that leads you astray each step of the way."

"The state in which I find myself is peculiar. I'm neither sick nor well. At times I'm pleased with my day at work, but then again suddenly, as if from nowhere, a sense of discontent creeps into my mind."

"You're an intelligent man, but at the same time you have a soft mind."

"What do you mean by a soft mind?" I asked.

"Soft in the sense that you are human," Father Theophilos replied. "To be human is to have feelings, to be unable to block out your emotions and live on reason alone. That's a blessing all creative people have, but at the same time it's a challenge, and sometimes a curse. The path is narrow and the Tempter lurks behind every tree, striking out at you when you least expect it. It's God's will that you pass this test and accomplish the task assigned to you."

"Do you mean that the sense of dissatisfaction is a signpost?"

"Yes. The discontent reminds you that you have neglected your inner self and that you should no longer suppress it," Father Theophilos explained. "Eventually it will rise to the surface, and if suppressed, it may develop into illness, infatuations, a passion for gambling or the craving for drink. When these passions burst loose, the voice of reason stands no chance. Therefore, you have to nip the thing in the bud."

"It seems that emotions steer the world. When you're overcome by emotions, wisdom flies out the window."

"How true," Father Theophilos agreed. "But we are also intellectual beings, and that is our salvation."

"But if reason cannot resist our emotions, how then can we be saved?"

"The intellect is not the same as the reason. Reason functions by formulating abstract concepts and then arguing on this basis and reaching a conclusion by virtue of deductive reasoning."

"Isn't that the same as being intellectual?" I asked, surprised.

"No!" His response was decisive. "No! The intellect is man's highest faculty. It dwells in the depths of the soul. It constitutes the innermost aspect of our heart. Provided that it is purified, we may know God, the inner essence, the principle of created things, by means of direct apprehension or spiritual perception. The intellect understands divine truth by means of immediate experience, intuition or so-called 'simple cognition.'"

"The aim of spiritual striving, then, is to cultivate our intellect?"

"Yes. It is only through our intellect that we can hope to identify the whisperings of the disguised Tempter, who unscrupulously targets the feelings of our emotional life."

"Spiritual striving is a means, then, not an end."

"This is why we shouldn't overdo it, because even that is the whisper of the devious devil." Father Theophilos struck a warning note. "God's mercy is not to be earned by some kind of asceticism and striving. Rather, what we need to do is regularly to cultivate our understanding."

"Is understanding the same as discernment?"

"Understanding requires discernment. Everyone is an unknown pilgrim to himself until he attains that understanding."

"But it's hidden!"

"Yes. Our understanding is hidden among thousands of weeds. This is why we must first strive to uproot the weeds and then to water our intellect. By increasing our understanding, we slow down the growth of the weeds. It's never completely brought to a standstill, however."

"The analogy with gardening and the uprooting of weeds is elucidating."

"It provides a positive mental picture of what spiritual striving is all about," Father Theophilos said. "Every time I tend my garden I conceive of it as increasing my discernment. Unceasing prayer and the act of pulling out the weed focuses my mind on the will of God."

"Aren't you ever afraid of fighting the demons all by yourself?"

"When I was young, I didn't like to be in the dark," he confessed. "On the Holy Mountain I sensed God's presence through experience. Since then I've had no fear of darkness."

"How did you rid yourself of the demonic whispers?"

"I didn't. At times the devil visits me daily. I'm not afraid of him, because the power of the Jesus Prayer eventually makes him leave me in peace. There's nothing the demons fear more than a man persistently praying in the name of our Lord. Nevertheless the devilish painters bother me with their innumerable tricks that manage to attract my attention and so distract me from the work I ought to be doing. My energies are consumed by fighting, and that's disturbing."

"Prayer, then, is the means to drive the demons away?"

"You shouldn't forget that our enemy is always lurking behind the corner, waiting for any new opportunity to strike," Father Theophilos warned me. "His tactic is to lull us into believing he's gone forever. As soon as we believe that, he strikes again, harder than ever."

"In my own work the striving is between the inner calling and other people's expectations," I said, and then explained: "I am convinced that everyone living in society has a special talent, which should, I think, be conceived of as his or her calling. For various reasons, we end up in circumstances that are unfavorable for pursuing that calling. We love comfort and therefore choose the realistic or easy path."

"We want to have everything at once. We want to become famous, we seek the esteem of other people and we want to have a perfect life in all respects."

"That's right. No patience at all. The slightest frustration is easily blown out of all proportion. Our expectations are too high. Therefore people end up divorcing for all the wrong reasons, only to regret it when it's too late."

"Mid-life is difficult enough here on the island," Father Theophilos assured me. "I can only imagine what it's like in society."

"Mid-life is the time in our life when we've experienced all the basics in life." I was thinking aloud. "Questions like 'Who am I?' and 'Where am I going?' begin to bother us. We dare not meet them head on. To avoid the anxiety they arouse, we throw ourselves into new adventures and affairs, with all this implies. Celebrities show us the way. Ordinary people follow like a flock of sheep."

"Not everyone is content with remarrying, changing jobs or taking up a new hobby, which they do in order to find immediate comfort in the stressful situation that mid-life anxiety causes.

Some people face the challenge with determination and begin to ask questions as anxiously as any child who wants to know this and that."

"Children never stop asking until they've understood the answer," I remarked.

"How true," Father Theophilos agreed. "In mid-life, like children we sense that there must be more to life than what we have seen and heard. This makes us more curious and eager to find out what lies behind what we are doing. We are all created by our Lord in his image. Over the years the wise man wants to find out more and more about himself, his image-likeness and his Creator."

"It takes a lifetime," I concluded.

"Searching is the answer," Father Theophilos replied. "We should learn to live a life of constant search, at rest and with the trustful mind of a child. Only our Lord knows the whole answer. At the hour of our death it is essential to be at peace with our life and with our Lord." His words comforted me.

"Narrow path, here I come!" I said in defiance. "If it implies fighting in the desert, so be it. I want to live life to the full, and not be constrained by prescribed roles. That may be my weakness."

"It's not a weakness, though being defiant is not the answer," Father Theophilos pointed out. "Your weakness is your strength. From the *Philokalia* we learn that in the front line of demons opposing us in our spiritual striving are those tempting us into gluttony. Then come those who put avaricious thoughts into our heads such as the desire for money, and those who incite us to seek the esteem of others. All the rest follow behind, and attack at the first opportunity, targeting those already wounded by one of the first three tempters. Their arsenal is unfailing. Their innumerable tricks of deception easily foil our efforts at spiritual striving."

"Are you saying that to choose the esteem and power of a civil servant instead of a life in creativity is to succumb to the Tempter's tricks?"

"If you have a calling, yes." Father Theophilos was adamant.

"It is next to impossible in everyday life to identify the Tempter's tricks among all that goes on around us," I continued.

"In everyday life things get blurred," was the response.

"Quite so. All your good intentions are forgotten. When I'm lost I notice my negligence and failure to keep on striving. How am I to stay on the path without constantly going astray? I ask myself this at times of despair. Returning to the path is always humiliating and frustrating. I find it hard to accept that I'll never attain my goal."

"It may be that treading the path is the goal," Father Theophilos suggested. "I, too, realize that time is running out. The idea of reaching a goal, of climbing a spiritual ladder and so forth, may be misleading, perhaps even one of the devil's tricks to distract us from properly exploring the path. We should focus only on spiritual striving at this very moment and not be concerned with the future. The future lies in the hands of our Lord. Our salvation is in his grace, not in our efforts," he concluded.

Father Theophilos had long since abandoned the mentality of a *streber*, the idea that the end justifies the means. At one point during my first days on the island I began to wonder whether he was a spiritual striver after all. He seemed so easy-going. Merrily we ate and drank wine together, and apart from the services and the unceasing praying while working, which he kept to rigorously, his daily routines did not seem to me to be too austere. Maybe that surprised me. Life on the island was tough, but far from impossible. His way of striving seemed so relaxed, never-ending like the waves lapping the shore, effortless and eternal. The divine rhythm had shaped his character and he seemed so much at peace that I started to doubt his sincerity until I was struck by his serenity. He was a spiritual virtuoso and therefore what he did seemed effortless. I found it easy to live in his company, but I very much doubted that I would be able to live on the island alone for years as he has done. His character had been shaped by the will of God, and as I jot this down in my diary I can see that my striving also begins to leave tracks in the form of verbal expressions of inner thoughts and understanding. I leave traces of an inner struggle on the pages of my diary. In the course of time the traces multiply and I have noticed how I have gone round in circles. In this sense, the diary is an excellent compass in our search for the path and for keeping to it. This is one of the lessons I have learned on the island so far. I am grateful for it and I will always keep Father Theophilos in my prayers.

Divina Laterna

I

O N MY LAST DAY ON THE ISLAND, Father Theophilos called me from my sleep as every other day by knocking rhythmically on my door. To my surprise he cut the morning service short. Then he explained to me that we had run out of fish. Fishing thus became the first duty of the day.

He had prepared our equipment while I was still asleep. The only thing left for me to do was to carry the basket with the long line to the boat. The cave was so dark in the early morning that I could hardly see anything in spite of Father Theophilos' oil lamp. He warned me several times against stumbling and falling into the water on the narrow, uneven path. I followed him as best I could. He seemed to have no problem. He was used to finding his way in the darkness.

As our boat slowly glided out of the cave into the open sea, the bluish light on the horizon indicated that dawn was not far off. Nevertheless, the darkness persisted for quite some time as we laid the long line. I realized that we must have woken up very early. I had no watch, so the only way I could tell the time was by the sun. I rowed forward slowly as Father Theophilos let out the long line, hook by hook. Once the task was accomplished, we had our morning tea and ate some biscuits and grapes and the packed food he had prepared for us.

The sunrise at sea was beautiful beyond belief. The cool of the morning faded away as the sunbeams began to warm our stiff bodies with their sweet touch. As the sun rose well above the sea it became uncomfortably hot, and I quickly put on my yellowish cap to protect the incipient bald patch on the top of my head. Experience told me that the sun and the sea were a dangerous combination, and you really need to be careful not to burn. Sunstroke could be fatal. Father Theophilos watched my actions with some amusement. Then he said, "That cap does not go with your black clothes." He took out a black monk's cap from his bag and gave it to me. It had a red cross sewn on the front of it, an ordinary cap used by most Athonites.

"Take this," he said. "It's more appropriate. Black is the symbol of death. Here you're dead to the world and its temptations, like any hermit. Leave all your worldly worries aside for some time yet before you return."

I immediately put on the black cap. "How does it fit?" I asked, as if it mattered how I looked.

"Perfectly," was his reply.

As soon as we had finished our tea, Father Theophilos started the engine and brought us back to the beginning of the long line. The sea was as bright as a mirror, reflecting the increasing heat of the sun. The refreshing wind was a welcome guest during our brief return to the starting point. Because the sea was calm, I had no difficulty in rowing the boat slowly forward as Father Theophilos lifted the long line back into the basket. There were no fish on the first row of hooks.

"Our Lord puts our patience to the test," Father Theophilos stated laconically.

Then after a while I heard a splashing, and I could tell from the hermit's smiling face that there were fish coming aboard. And so it was. He threw fish after fish into the bucket before putting the hooks back into the basket. Everything was in order. When the bucket was full, he threw the rest of the fish back into the sea saying: "Enough for one day."

The sun was already quite strong and I felt somewhat dizzy. It was therefore a great relief to me when Father Theophilos finally steered the boat smoothly into the cave. A nice cool breeze greeted us from within as if from a huge fridge. I really needed it. My eyes were blinded, though, and I could hardly see anything. How he found his way in the darkness I do not know. Practice makes perfect, I suppose.

In turn we went up to the plateau in the lift. It was a miracle. The lift rose very slowly but steadily—simply a miracle. The fridge and the freezer were also driven by the solar energy. As soon as we stepped into the kitchen we started to clean the fish, and then we put them in the freezer. Having completed our work, we enjoyed our last lunch together, fresh fried fish, black olives, bread, tomatoes, water and a glass of wine. I really felt welcome in the *kellion*. Father Theophilos looked pleased at first, but then his face turned more stern. "Another week on the island is out of the question," he said. "Your duty is in the world."

He must have seen how content I felt, and wanted to make sure that I would not suggest prolonging my sojourn. His words surprised me though, which he also realized. He explained further. "You may come in a few years, but for the time being you're much needed in society. Your striving is in the world, not here."

"Society is my destiny," I sighed. I was not yet ready to return to the cruel world and all its everyday worries.

"Don't despair. Always keep in mind the image of the pilgrim en route."

Father Theophilos poured another glass of wine and then continued: "A pilgrim's journey is long. It lasts a lifetime. It is imperative, therefore, that you follow the strict rhythm of a spiritual striver in the world. It requires self-discipline. The desert fathers talk about sobriety."

"For years I have tried to resist offers that distract me from reaching my goal."

"The task of a striver is to fulfil God's will," Father Theophilos once more reminded me. "That's your goal as well. You strive with your ascetic pen, I with my gardening. Both are of equal importance, because our Lord has given us different gifts and talents to be used in His glory."

"In the world, being distracted and losing your way are everyday events."

"It's exactly the same here on the island," Father Theophilos assured me. "The strict daily rhythm aside, you have to keep a close watch on the thoughts that pop up from within."

"These thoughts are so deceptive. They sneak in. I act upon them and only afterwards do I realize the deception."

"This is why you should keep a diary, so you will be able to follow the thought patterns for a longer time and learn to identify the tricks of the Deluder. Even if you fall, don't despair. Despair is one of the devil's tricks. Take up the fight with even stronger determination."

"The fathers speak about discernment. I understand it to be a special faculty or gift to distinguish between the different kinds of thoughts that enter our minds."

"Yes, it is. We need to assess them accurately and treat them accordingly. Spiritual discernment is a gift that enables us to distinguish between thoughts or sometimes visions inspired by God and the innumerable suggestions, even fantasies, placed enticingly in front of us by the devil."

"Can I also apply this knowledge in society?"

"Of course. Following your inner calling is God's will, while the expectations and demands put on you by society are often the devil's work, meant to lead you astray. But," he emphasized, "it's not that easy. What you consider to be God's will may equally well be the work of a demon."

"How can I know for sure?"

"You can't. Humility is the word. Time and again you have to listen to the will of God. It's the eye or lantern of the soul, by which we find our way along the spiritual path without falling into extremes. It's not what we enjoy and esteem that should be our guide, but the voice that speaks against our fixed ideas and vainglory."

"So I can't even trust what I consider to be my own calling?"

"No you can't. However, you should ask yourself if the calling provides you with a unique opportunity. Is it really a once-in-a-lifetime change? When you consider whether the calling is in fact a temptation, you should also ask yourself whether you want to follow the calling merely for the calling's sake, or whether it is the anticipated reward that makes you so interested in accomplishing the task. Is it the reward, the power or the esteem of other people that lurk behind your enthusiasm?"

"Temptations recur."

"Indeed they do. You will easily identify the pattern from the notes in your diary. And remember, if you fall, which is human and happens to all of us, you should not fall into despair. In recognizing the first sneaking feelings of despair you will be able to show how brave a Christian soldier you are before the enemy. Thousands of hermits have endured that situation. I try hard to follow in their footsteps, and you must also do your best."

"A life-time is all too short for this kind of battle."

"Spiritual striving is like catching a fish by the tail. The fish is slippery and the task is next to impossible. Therefore it's a blessing that our salvation is dependent not on our own efforts, but on the mercy of God. If it were up to us, I fear nobody would be saved."

"When I'm writing I have the feeling that the words are slipping away just like a fish when I'm about to catch it. I almost have it within my grip, but then suddenly it's gone."

"You can never catch anything so slippery by the tail," Father Theophilos assured me. "However, you shouldn't worry about that. The tail serves as a signpost. It informs you that you're on the right path. You should not concern yourself with the fact that you cannot catch the tail, but follow its lead, though not blindly. The Deluder may also appear in the form of a tail leading you astray. Take a break! Recite the Jesus Prayer, and the detached point of view reached through prayer will help you to see clearly again."

After this intense discussion both of us felt tired. We had woken up in the early hours, and the fresh air at sea and the spiritual striving had used all our energy. I could hear Father Theophilos praying in his cell as I lay on my bed. "Lord Jesus Christ, have mercy on us." He prayed in the plural and I felt blessed. I knew that he would also be remembering me in his prayers in the future, and that comforted me. What more can one ask than to be remembered in this way?

2

AFTER THE EVENING SERVICE, Father Theophilos took me completely by surprise by taking me to a tower at the top of a steep cliff. Well before sunset we climbed the steep path cut between two mountain tops behind the house. The tower was built of the same stone as the cliff so that it was hard to detect from the plateau. From the sea it simply looked like part of the mountain. As we climbed we prayed unceasingly: "Lord Jesus Christ, have mercy on us."

The steps were narrow and steep. There was a simple iron chain on the right-hand side fastened to the rock for safety, but it did not make me feel any better. Father Theophilos could sense my fear from the accelerating pace of my prayer as, with some apprehension, I followed in his footsteps. I did not dare to look down, although I am not normally afraid of heights. I thought it better not to push my luck and take risks—vertigo can strike at any moment and the steep steps seemed hazardous enough to me. Finally, after a fifteen-minute climb, we stood outside the entrance on a small landing. The view was breathtaking. We were literally standing between heaven and earth, like eagles on the edge of the highest cliff.

"Don't worry!" Father Theophilos comforted me. "The descent will be easier. Simply follow in my footsteps."

He opened the door of the tower with a huge old key and I was relieved to enter the small hall. It was much smaller inside than I had expected and the thick walls took up most of the space. Everything inside was made of wood. As we climbed the stairs I realized that there were four floors altogether, each with two small rooms. The tower had served as a refuge in medieval times, where the hermits could keep all their valuables and food safe from the pirates who regularly sailed these waters.

The top floor had a small hall with a table and three chairs. It served as a narthex to the other room, which was a chapel. Father Theophilos lit the oil lamp, we crossed ourselves and kissed the icons in turn, then composed ourselves in prayer. When we returned to the hall he told me that he saw the chapel as a divine lantern. *Divina laterna* was the Latin expression he used.

"I'm sure you noticed that the tower is camouflaged by the cliffs and by the material it is built of," he said as we sat by the table. "It can't be seen from the plateau nor from the sea. It's difficult to detect even from the air, except late in the evening or at night when the oil lamps reflect light through the narrow windows."

"It's very cleverly constructed." I was impressed.

"The tower can't be seen, but it still exists." Father Theophilos was triumphant. "We can see in all directions through the windows. Although our Lord may seem to be completely out of sight, even dead to some people, he is constantly watching over us. Whenever the Deluder bothers me, I turn my face towards this divine lantern. Although I don't see it from my house, I still know it exists. It flashes like a lighthouse, a guide par excellence like the icon of the Mother of God or the Forerunner."

"*Divina laterna*," I repeated. "This is a perfect lookout tower."

The view from the small rectangular window was stunning beyond words. The sea glittered in the sunset like a million diamonds. For the first time in my life, or at least for as long as I can remember, I experienced a sweet inner peace of mind. Not even in church or in the chapel had I ever felt this way.

To be at the center of the divine lantern was odd. Can a pilgrim ever be in a more sacred place? Was this the message in the dream that urged me to visit this monastic island? Being at peace in sacred surroundings is an unforgettable experience. May the tower be the signpost of my life, the divine lantern of my soul, throwing light on the path I should follow.

"You can see a long way from here, can't you?" Father Theophilos interrupted my introspection.

"All the way to the horizon," I replied.

"When I came here, an old Russian hermit called Father Nikon had been living on the island since the revolution," he told me. "He had been a young officer in the Tsar's army. During the turbulent year of the revolution, he fled to the Russian monastery of Panteleimon on the Holy Mountain. After spending some time there he became a monk, and then ended up here as a hermit."

"Did you often visit him?"

"When he fell ill he couldn't live alone any more. Many younger monks from the Holy Mountain sojourned here from time to time, helping him with his daily routines. In return he was their spiritual father, advising them in their striving towards deification. By accident I happened to be here when he died. No, not by accident. It was God's will."

"It must have been quite an experience."

"It was frightening at first," Father Theophilos confessed, "but Father Nikon had the gift of clairvoyance. With his inner eye he saw how troubled I was in having to take care of his remains, so he gave me all the necessary instructions for his burial and then passed away, completely at ease as the air slowly came out of his nostrils at his last breath."

Father Theophilos' eyes moistened a little as he remembered his last spiritual father, and after some minutes of silence I asked him: "Where did you bury him?"

"In the small cemetery uphill," he replied. "However, his last wish was for his skull to be placed in this tower next to the skulls of all the other holy men. He had experienced the most joyful moments of his life sitting by this table."

"But you buried him in the graveyard. How did the skull end up here?"

"After three years we dug up the grave, cleaned the bones with wine, put them in a box and then took the skull." Father Theophilos rose from his chair, went to the cupboard by the wall, opened the door and took Father Nikon's skull from the end of a row of skulls lined up like books on a shelf. On the forehead there was a cross, the capital letter N and the years 1896-1981 inscribed for identification.

"This is the skull of Father Nikon," Father Theophilos said, then kissed it and showed it to me. "I'll join the row in due course. He was a most humble spiritual striver. In his presence I felt at home, completely at ease."

Taken by surprise, I immediately made the sign of the cross, and then kissed the skull. Although I had seen many skulls on the Holy Mountain, there was something awesome in the situation. Father Theophilos must have noticed that I felt a bit awkward.

"It's the most natural thing for the skulls to be kept here in the divine lantern," he explained. "They are safe from any possible intruder, not that there have been any in recent centuries."

"Between heaven and earth," I mused. "It's as natural as can be."

At nightfall, in the light of the oil lamp, the skull looked frightening. Perhaps it was the play of the shadows or the archetypal fears from deep inside me that came to the surface. In one sense it was sacrilege, but then again it was not. This was the custom in all of the monasteries on the Holy Mountain. The elder Silouan's ascetic formula came to mind, "Keep your mind in hell, and despair not." The fear of death may be worse than death itself, and I felt a sudden togetherness with the remains of Father Nikon. His body was dead, but he was present. I cannot explain how. Something of him was present for a brief moment and all my fears disappeared.

"Lord Jesus Christ, have mercy on us," Father Theophilos prayed before he put the skull back into the cupboard. Spontaneously I also prayed for mercy.

When Father Theophilos returned to his chair by the table he looked at me and said,

"*Nomen est omen!* René means 'reborn.' You're now at that crossroads in your life."

"Yes."

"Your studies have undoubtedly taught you that the reasons for going on a pilgrimage often have nothing to do with reason. In the West, man is generally considered to be a rational being, *animal rationale* is the old Latin expression. However, this is misleading. Our emotions rule our lives."

"Indeed. We need to learn the movements of our thoughts and emotions, if we wish to find the key to happiness and a healthy life."

"It's imperative to realize that our life and life on earth is part of a much bigger scheme, a divine plan. All too often we get stuck on the details and on our own present comfort."

"Isn't it important to seize the moment though?" I asked, somewhat confused by this statement.

"The moments are parts of a larger plan," he repeated. "Our Lord has given all of us a divine and unique talent. All life is designed to follow a purpose. However, it's up to us whether we recognize that purpose and take up the challenge to fulfil it."

"In principle this is easy, but as you know, in practice it's next to impossible."

"Don't listen to the demon of distrust," Father Theophilos warned me. "The dilemma facing us humans is that, although the will to do good is there, the ability is not. The good we want to do, we fail to do, but the wrong we don't want to do, we still do. Therefore, to get things into proportion, we need to have the whole scenario in sight all the time."

"A sense of proportion is indeed elementary."

"People who have survived serious accidents usually pay less attention to details. It is a miracle to be alive and they don't want to waste their time crying over minor losses or setbacks. These are simply part of life."

"Yes. Life is all too short to focus on trivialities. In the heat of the everyday battle we tend to blow things out of proportion."

"That's the problem," Father Theophilos agreed. "Therefore we need the divine lantern to give us the right direction and show us the reefs. In life as on the sea, it is of vital importance to keep a log book. It's the only means by which we can check our route each night and correct it if necessary."

"By keeping a diary one cultivates a feeling for language. You are constantly in search of the right word. You speak the word aloud to listen to how it sounds. Does it sound right? This is the way to open up the universe of the word, all its meanings, the subtle nuances as well as their etymological roots and ramifications."

"Renéos, this is the heart of the matter. To write is to cultivate one's feeling for the word, *logos* as we say here in Greece, the spoken word. In the Gospel we can read exactly this, 'In the beginning the Word already was. The Word was in God's presence, and what God was, the Word was.' To understand the Word, therefore, is to sense the presence of God's will."

"Sensing the message in the word is difficult. This is why I decided not to become a writer. It's more likely than not to fail."

"Oh my dear Renéos," Father Theophilos exclaimed, "you are speaking with the voice of the demon of distrust. Be confident and patient, and always keep in mind the reward of having done your duty. With the help of our Lord you simply cannot fail. It may be difficult, and may even take a long time to accomplish, but eventually you will succeed. You're a pilgrim, aren't you? You can't remain unknown to yourself. When you return to your daily duties remember to keep this watchtower in mind. Everything will turn out well in the end." I felt comforted.

We had been sitting at the table in the light of the oil lamp for quite some time. The sun had set and the moon had risen once more, reflecting its silvery bridge towards the tower. Father Theophilos lit another lamp and we began our descent back to the *kellion*. For safety reasons I followed close behind him. In the dark it was difficult to find the step, and he kept holding the oil lamp all the time so that I could see the way down. It was a risky venture. We rested for a while half way down. He asked me to look up at the tower and to remember the twinkling light of the oil lamp he had left burning by the window. "Twinkle, twinkle little star," he recited with a smile. His humour encouraged me and all my fear of heights was swept away.

"Remember Renéos," he advised me, "no wind is favorable for someone who cannot decide where to sail. May the *divina laterna* guide you in your everyday life."

The light twinkling joyfully in the total darkness warmed my heart. We continued our descent to the *kellion* in a state of inner bliss, at least I did. Before I went to bed I carefully jotted down all my experiences, because I wanted to make sure not to forget anything. Exhausted by the excitement of the day, I went to bed, but the twinkling light kept appearing in my visual memory. I took this to mean good-night, and after praying, "Lord Jesus Christ, have mercy on me," I finally fell sound asleep.

3

ON THE MORNING OF MY DEPARTURE, after the morning service and the monastic breakfast, we waited for Christos on the balcony. The sea was calm like the day before, and the weather forecast was that this day would be warm and sunny too. Then it would turn cooler.

"Keep to your resolve," Father Theophilos said as we sipped our morning coffee. "You've decided to embark on the narrow path. Don't forget that habit is second nature. By observing a semi-ascetic daily rhythm you'll smoothe the path."

"I'll try my best," I assured him. "So far I've sailed the sea and kept the instructions in an unopened letter. Now that I've read some of the advice sealed within it, I'll try to make the best of it."

"You can always get in touch with me through Christos," Father Theophilos reassured me. "If you would like to return for a another sojourn in a few years, I'll be glad to have you as my guest."

"*Géronda*, I am ever so grateful. This promise means the world to me."

The connection and friendship between us pleased me as nothing had before. I have met many monks in my life, and only a few have known how to put themselves in my shoes. They live in a world of their own. Little do they care about the problems in society other than in prayer, where they ask for our Lord's mercy. To be fair, they pray for the wellbeing of the whole world, Orthodox and the rest. Nevertheless, the worries of a middle-aged family man are not their highest priority. I was often told, "Why don't you come here and live as a monk? Our Lord will see to it that you won't lack anything."

"Look," Father Theophilos interrupted my thoughts. "Christos is approaching the island."

I could see nothing at first, but then when Father Theophilos pointed out where to look, I noticed a tiny boat in the midst of the glittering waves. We went immediately with the wheelbarrow to the lift. One at a time we descended to the cave, where we waited for Christos. The opening was so small that when the boat finally glided through it, the cave became completely dark since there was no light at all except that reflected though the water.

"*Eulogíte*" Christos greeted us as he landed on the jetty.

"*O Kyrios*," Father Theophilos replied.

When we had carried all the supplies to the *kellion*, Christos told us that a friend of his was to bring fresh water for a month or so by army helicopter the following weekend. The rain water was drinkable after it had been boiled, but there is no denying that fresh bottled water tastes much better.

"Have you enjoyed your stay?" Christos asked me when all the supplies had been put away.

"It's been wonderful."

I was going to tell him more, but Father Theophilos interrupted me by giving a full report of the events of the week. Christos smiled with contentment.

When Christos had kissed the icon of St. Nicholas, we had lunch. The weather forecast promised a stormy wind for the next day, so as soon as we had eaten we began our voyage back to Ouranoupolis. Christos was eager to return before the wind rose. It is always dangerous at sea this time of the year.

On the jetty, before I went on board, I kissed Father Theophilos' hand, as is customary. As is also customary, he withdrew his hand a little as a sign of humility. He then blessed me and our voyage, and said that the divine lantern would be our lighthouse in the world. It will guide us through our everyday troubles and worries. As a sign of his blessing, he pushed the boat away from the jetty. It went smoothly out of the cave. Since the water was a bit higher, we had to bend down at the entrance so as not to hit our heads against the rock. So began our voyage back into the world.

The sea was still calm, but a gentle breeze came up now and again, a sign that a storm was on its way. We had a favorable wind and the voyage took us only four hours. All the same, there was enough time for me to reflect upon my experiences on the monastic island.

The island existed. Father Theophilos existed. He was well and very spiritual indeed. The dream proved to be true and it had been worth following. But what now? What was waiting for me in Finland? These were questions many a pilgrim has asked himself since medieval times. Why go back? Quite a few never do. They leave their families and loved ones for a life in their new homeland, some fantastic place they fell in love with during their journey. They literally begin a new life and nothing is heard from them again. Some, of course, die of illnesses or other misfortunes, but it is apparent from the records at the pilgrimage centers that quite a few simply decide not to go home. Why, then, should I?

It is really tempting to stay in Greece, in Ouranoupolis for example. It would be quite possible for me. Living would not be too expensive, and I could earn money by teaching or writing. The whispers of the Tempter are enticing. Why not? There are many good reasons for staying here.

Then I pulled myself together. What is waiting for me at home? The struggle against a bureaucracy at the university and the pressure of perpetual evaluation and assessment. "Publish or perish" used to be the slogan. Now it is "produce or perish," producing referring to taking full responsibility for students earning their degrees within the prescribed time, playing an active role in raising funds for the university, and being in the front line of one's subject of research. It is impossible to fulfil all these expectations. It is depressing to struggle against the *Zeitgeist*, the political spirit of the age in our European universities. Why should I bother?

My children are already grown up and away from home, studying at other universities. They cannot understand my dilemma. When you have your whole life in front of you, you are enthusiastic about everything, about every new experience, life is simply smiling at you and you are smiling along with it. The questions that occupy my mind are a million miles away from their daily lives. It will take many years before they are in my situation. That is just as well.

My parents are fighting their illnesses, which occupy most of their thoughts. They are living their lives in slow motion, one task at a time. It would be wrong for me to bother them with my concerns. I have to allow them to believe that I am strong and well so that they can prepare for their departure in peace. They need that quality time, and it is not right for me to take that illusion away from them.

I cannot talk about these things with my colleagues either, because we are in the same boat and everyone wants to keep up appearances. The saying, "no one understands me" seems as true as ever.

A drowning man will clutch at a straw. What is my straw? My wife! Although she also has a demanding job, she has always given me the freedom to follow my inner spiritual path, and has been there for me every time the darkest clouds have hidden the sun from me. She is the reason for my going back. The best qualities are combined in her: *belle sensuelle* and *femme inspiratrice*. With her support I will find wisdom: *sophía*.

4

BEFORE MY DEPARTURE FROM Ouranoupolis, I went to see Christos to thank him for everything he had done for me. We had our last cup of coffee together on his balcony, watching the sunrise as so many time before. Farewells are always a little melancholy.

"Are you satisfied with your journey?" he asked.

"More than satisfied. I'm thrilled, thanks to you."

"*Típota* ("That's nothing")," he replied. "*Géronda* is the most spiritual father I know. He's modest, he loves solitude, but when he decides to take in a guest he is sociable beyond belief. He has a very warm heart. He will most certainly remember you in his daily prayers."

"I'll need it."

"Many years ago, when I was having a difficult time in my life, and when the demon of despair had me in its grip, Father Theophilos encouraged me by giving me words of advice of an old Japanese samurai who had taught his pupil to prepare for the coming fight:

> If you think that you're going to win,
> you've lost.
> If you are afraid of losing,
> you've lost.
> If you pay attention to the size of your enemy,
> you've lost.
> If you underestimate your enemy's talent,
> you've lost.
> If you doubt your own abilities,
> you've lost.
> If you're arrogant,
> you've lost.

If you're afraid,
  you've lost.
What is left? you ask.
The fight!
Focus on that only!

I was stunned. What could I say? After a moment of silence, Christos explained.

"That is how broad-minded *géronda* really is. These days he considers himself a Christian soldier who is fighting demons. Like David, he's not afraid of the size of the devilish Goliaths. He focuses only on the fight. With his Jesus Prayer he drives away all the deluders and tempters. He's afraid of nothing, because with the mercy of our Lord the devil stands no chance."

The morning hours at Christos' house passed all too quickly. We were so absorbed in our discussion that I nearly missed the bus. A feeling of nostalgia come over me as looked out of the window while the bus went down the main street in the village and then along the coastline of the peninsula. My return was as irrevocable as the challenge of the task ahead was unavoidable. I was heading for an old struggle, but with new resources. The function of our striving in the world is not only to progress in our careers. My principal aim was to become acquainted with the unknown pilgrim in me by coping with the distractions and temptations in the world. I was to tame the monsters of daily drudgery at the university. After my sojourn on the monastic island I was well prepared for that. All my doubts had been swept away. I felt filled with an inner certainty, because on the monastic island the "favouring breezes, instantly the tempest ceases, and to rest the sea was laid."

COLOPHON

The Unknown Pilgrim

Written by René Gothóni

Text designed and typeset by the monks of the

Monastery of Saint John of San Francisco

Manton, California

Typeset in Adobe Caslon Pro, 12 point on 14.25 point

2006

To God be the glory,
now and ever,
and unto ages of ages.

Amen.

DIVINE
ASCENT
PRESS

PRINTED AND BOUND IN THE UNITED STATES OF AMERICA
BY VERSA PRESS, INC.